"For men who realize there is a better way to live but need help in discovering it . . . For those of us who were, like most men, "raised to work not to relate," Robert Pasick goes beyond the usual clinical anecdotes to reveal practical lessons and to deliver a real step-by-step, you-can-do-it book. I highly recommend it. Furthermore, I fervently wish every man would read it and embrace its lessons. We could make not only our lives but the world a better place."

—James Autry, author of *Love and Profit*

"An interesting approach to an important problem in our time. Pasick makes us sit up and take notice of our shortcomings as human beings."

—Ernie Harwell, Hall of Fame broadcaster for the Detroit Tigers

"In this clear and well-written book, Dr. Pasick provides a blend of real-life stories and intellectual framework that will help men both feel and think."

—Warren Farrell, Ph.D., author of *Why Men Are the Way They Are*

"Vitally rich in its readability, clarity and insights, *Awakening from the Deep Sleep* offers men a guide for real change. Pasick truly knows the lives of men and understands their relationships with the women in their lives. A must read for women as well!"

—Marilyn Mason, author of *Making Our Lives Our Own*

AWAKENING FROM THE DEEP SLEEP

AWAKENING FROM THE DEEP SLEEP

A POWERFUL GUIDE FOR COURAGEOUS MEN

ROBERT S. PASICK, PH.D.

HarperSanFrancisco

A Division of HarperCollins*Publishers*

The first-person stories and case examples in the book accurately reflect the feelings, experiences, and circumstances expressed by clients, their families, and friends; but all names, locales, and identifying details have been changed.

AWAKENING FROM THE DEEP SLEEP: *A Powerful Guide for Courageous Men.* Copyright © 1992 by Robert S. Pasick, Ph.D. All rights reserved. Printed in the United States of America. No part of this book may be used or reproduced in any manner whatsoever without written permission except in the case of brief quotations embodied in critical articles and reviews. For information address HarperCollins Publishers, 10 East 53rd Street, New York, NY 10022.

FIRST EDITION

Library of Congress Cataloging-in-Publication Data
Pasick, Robert S.
    Awakening from the deep sleep : a powerful guide for courageous men / Robert S. Pasick.—1st Harper Collins ed.
        p.   cm.
    ISBN 0-06-250694-3 (alk. paper)
    1. Middle aged men—Psychology.   2. Masculinity (Psychology)   3. Middle aged men—Psychology—Case studies.
    4. Masculinity (Psychology)—Case studies.   I. Title.
    BF692.5.P375 1992
    155.6'6—dc20

    93 94 95 96 HAD 10 9 8 7 6 5 4

To my parents, Irma and Al
To Daniel and Adam
To Pat
and to the memory of Izzie
with love

CONTENTS

ACKNOWLEDGMENTS

First and foremost I wish to thank my wife, Patricia Carino Pasick, for her significant contributions to the development of my ideas about men and gender. Throughout the twenty-five years of our relationship she has helped me redefine the meaning of being a man. Without her support and encouragement this project would have been impossible. Likewise I thank my two sons, Adam and Daniel, for their patience, good cheer, and insights, which have enlightened my understanding about what it means to be a man.

I also thank my lucky stars for John Bacon, my writing consultant, whose wisdom, heartfelt support, and friendship have been essential to my ability to finish the book. Barbara Moulton, my editor at Harper San Francisco, has been marvelous at every step in the process. I am convinced that she is not only a great editor but a gifted psychologist as well. I am grateful, too, for my agent, Ellen Levine, who believed in me early on and has encouraged me throughout.

I have received wonderful and cheerful administrative assistance from many talented people, including Cindy Davis, Kathi Nelson, Linda Hall, Kit Dickinson, and Marie Murrel. I am especially indebted to Nancy Yonkman and Chris Pearson, who helped me at the end of the project when my energy was running low.

I am quite fortunate to work with great colleagues at the Ann Arbor Center for the Family. All have contributed ideas and support. Thank you, Brian Ashin, Pat Campbell, Fernando Colon, Doug Ensor, Paul Estensen, Judith Kleinman, Pat Pasick, Ellen Taylor, Mary Whiteside, Chris White and especially Jo Allen and Sylvia Gordon. Special thanks, too, to Marilyn Mason, who introduced me to the folks at Harper San Francisco, and to Barry and Eileen Gordon, my longtime best friends, who have been tremendous sources of support throughout my career. Thanks to Dick Schwartz and Sylvia Hacker for their useful suggestions.

Last, and most important, I wish to express my gratitude to the men I have worked with in therapy over the past several years. They have been my true inspiration. Theirs are the courageous stories I endeavor to tell in this book. I hope I've gotten it right, guys!

AWAKENING
FROM THE
DEEP
SLEEP

You Know You're in the Deep Sleep When...

1. You describe your life as hectic, busy, or rushed.

2. You depend on your mate to tell you how you feel.

3. Work is more enjoyable or rewarding than your home is.

4. You distance yourself from feeling any intense emotions.

5. You have trouble saying "I don't know" or "I'm not sure."

6. You keep secrets from your wife because you don't want to upset her.

7. You are guarded around other men.

8. You have lost interest in sex with your mate.

9. You have only two feelings: good and bad.

10. You think it's your responsibility to fix your wife's problems.

11. You are more comfortable talking openly to women than to men.

12. You believe you can turn your emotions on and off at will.

13. You have trouble talking about hurts from the past.

14. You've considered entering therapy but think it would be a sign of weakness.

15. You want to reconnect with your father but don't know how.

16. You constantly compare yourself to other men to see how well you measure up.

17. You are fixated on earning more and more money.

18. You question whether you still love your wife.

19. You depend on your mate to arrange your social life.

20. You ignore pain, thinking it will go away on its own.

21. You feel fenced in by your mate.

22. You fear your mate will leave you.

23. You feel ambivalent about or even hostile to the women's movement.

24. You are not sure what you really want.

25. Your life feels out of balance.

1

Falling Into the Deep Sleep

This book tells the story of the challenges men currently face as we cope with the shift in men's and women's roles that has taken place over the past twenty years. Whether it is sex, marriage, work, children, aging, divorce, or caring for elderly parents, our traditional roles are being continually redefined. Although men now in their midyears have been at the crux of these changes, we are often ill-equipped to make the transition from one role to the next. The moment we seem to adapt to one major change, we are presented with the next one.

I am a man much like the men I describe in this book. I am forty-five with two children, ages thirteen and sixteen, a working wife, and two parents in their seventies. I have a good job, a nice house, live in a pleasant neighborhood in a fine American town. I am privileged and fortunate. But am I happy in my role as a man? At times I am not sure.

The men I see in my practice as a psychologist come to me because they are not happy. When they apprehensively call me on the phone for an appointment, they are not sure what their problems are or how to solve them. They often interpret the very act of calling a psychologist for help as an admission of failure as a man. We're supposed to be able to handle problems on our own. Real men, after all, should be invulnerable, independent, strong.

This book is about men who have admitted their vulnerability. They have entrusted me with their stories and have given me permission to tell you about them. They want other men and women to be able to share their experiences.

Who are these men? What kinds of problems have led them to seek out therapy? What has the experience been like for them? Let me begin by describing six such men.

They sat nervously in my office, eyeing one another as if to size up their relative roles in the men's group I had asked them to join. Making small talk about the weather and basketball kept their minds off their apprehension. In a few minutes they would be expected to share intimate thoughts and feelings with one another.

For most of them, being in individual or marital therapy had been difficult enough. They could recall the sense of failure they had experienced when they had to call on a therapist for help. The six were relieved to find that the first question I asked addressed their fears directly: "How does being in a group with other men fit with your conceptions of what it means to be a man?"

Scott, a forty-two-year-old lawyer wearing khaki slacks and a blue denim shirt, started out eagerly by explaining that he had always been taught that being a man meant being self-reliant. For years he had hesitated to go to therapy because he believed that he should solve his problems on his own. Only when his wife threatened to leave him did Scott reluctantly agree to accompany her to see a therapist. "Even then she had to take me along kicking and screaming," he said.

Phil, a forty-four-year-old teacher, said the hardest thing for him had been facing his fear. "All my life my father told me to keep a stiff upper lip," he said. "I was never supposed to let anyone know when things were bothering me. I remember one time as a kid when I backed away from a fight and told Dad about it. He got mad at me because I was afraid of getting beat up. I never let my dad know I was afraid again. Part of coming to therapy for me was having to admit that I couldn't by myself handle all the stresses I was having on the job."

For Tom entering the group meant facing a more immediate fear. For most of his thirty-five years he had been struggling with his sexual identity. After a futile attempt at marriage and constant struggles with alcoholism, he had decided to be open about his homosexuality. He was aware that he would be the only gay member of the group but had decided that exploring his feelings about male friendships, his father, and his own sexual preference was worth the risk. "The hardest part of entering this group for me is wondering how these other men will react to me," he said.

Derrick, thirty-three, also had much to fear about the group. As its only black member, he wondered if he would be accepted. Throughout his whole life he had felt tremendous pressure to conform to a strict image that equated manliness with machismo. To join a therapy group — a group composed of white middle-class men, where he knew he would have to take risks involving self-revelation — went against everything Derrick had learned about protecting himself as a male in American society. Derrick had climbed out of poverty, worked his way through college, and was now near the end of dental school. This struggle had required immense self-reliance, which was hard to reconcile with exposing one's psyche to a group of strangers.

Mike, a union carpenter, had grave doubts about being there, too. As he sipped his coffee, he wondered whether he fit at all with the men in the room. To him they seemed more sophisticated; they used big words and fancy concepts. Mike saw himself as a simple man who had gotten ahead in the world by keeping his nose to the grindstone. Now, at age fifty-three, he recognized that he was in trouble. His daughter had been diagnosed with a severe chronic illness, and Mike was having difficulty coping with it. His daughter's social worker had suggested the group, and Mike agreed to try it. But as an independent man, he never felt comfortable in group settings or in being open with men.

Arnie, forty-eight, was dressed more formally than the other men. His expensive suit belied his humble origins in rural Kentucky. He had joined the navy, gone to college on the G.I. Bill, then worked his way through medical school. His cool, aloof attitude toward the group mirrored his relationship to his wife, and probably to his patients as well. He, too, had started therapy at the urging of his wife, who had grown increasingly frustrated with his lack of warmth, especially after the last of their three children left home.

Arnie hoped that the other men might give him some ideas on how to change. "I know I'm on the cold side," he explained, "but that's just the way I was raised. I love my wife and want to stay married. She's a career woman, an organizational consultant. I know she wants more from me, but I don't know how to give her what she wants. She says I don't listen to her, and she's right. But I just can't seem to change my ways." As Arnie said these words to the strangers in the group, he knew he was taking a big risk. As a doctor, he always managed to stay in a one-up position.

Now, as he revealed his fear of losing his wife, he could no longer hide behind the status of his white coat.

This book tells the stories of such men and the process of change that I describe as awakening from the deep sleep. The "deep sleep" is an emotional, cognitive, and behavioral state that many men drift into as a consequence of striving to grow up male in Western society. Manhood is not a one-time developmental milestone. It is not enough to prove oneself a man and then be done with it. Rather manhood is a status that must be earned repeatedly. We can be a "man" one moment and be considered weak (or not a man) the next if we fail to meet some challenge.

Growing up male requires that we learn the rules of a game we are only vaguely aware of playing, and to win at it. We must be self-sufficient, rational, and action oriented. From the time we were young we learned to compare ourselves with other boys according to strict criteria to see who was the "better man"— and to distinguish our behavior from that of girls. Hiding "unmanly" impulses often became our major preoccupation as boys. Most men have painful memories of times they unwittingly displayed "feminine" behavior. Rick, a forty-six-year-old real estate broker, remembers coming home crying when he was eight because a dog had bitten him. His father laughed at him for being so upset over such a minor incident. His dad then explained that the dog had bitten him because somehow Rick had let the dog know he was scared. Rick learned this lesson: Adhering to the masculine code not only averts the scorn of important men but even impresses dogs by its strength.

This process of sorting out masculine from feminine traits was all the more confusing because men and women often responded to boys quite differently. Our mothers may have encouraged our creativity when we were making up stories or drawing, but our fathers probably took a dim view of such behavior. Our fathers and coaches inspired us to make hard tackles playing football, while our mothers may have worried about our safety.

Life became a process of following a script that taught us how to be men. It was like going down a road without a clearly defined midline. On one side was a set of prescriptions that defined manly behavior. On the other side were nonmanly or "sissy" behaviors. If we forgot what we were doing, if we became distracted and followed an inclination to wander over to the other side to explore something interesting, we would find ourselves on the wrong side — the feminine side — and if other boys or men saw us there, we would be embarrassed. We would be called names and made to feel ashamed. Our own manhood would be called into question.

Consequently we strove to learn the rules, often through a painful process of trial and error. Slowly we learned which set of actions, thoughts, and feelings would be most likely to keep us on the correct side of the road. As we grew older, we became clearer about the rules of the game. We learned which parts to develop and which parts to suppress; which feelings to vent and which to hide; which people to associate with and which to shun.

Through the socialization process of growing up male we learned to adhere to a set of beliefs about how to act as men. The belief system certainly may have varied somewhat depending on ethnicity, family background, and social class, but to a large extent these beliefs were remarkably universal. Although most men have not been aware of these beliefs on a conscious level, we have felt their powerful impact from childhoon on. The beliefs generally look like this:

TEN CENTRAL MANDATES OF MANHOOD

1. We must be self-reliant.
2. We should be competitive in all endeavors.
3. We should not reveal our fears.
4. We should be in control of ourselves at all times.
5. We need to be cautious about getting too close to anyone because intimacy weakens self-reliance and control.
6. We should focus on achieving power and success.
7. When we encounter a problem, we should be able to fix it through action.
8. We should keep score and always know where we stand relative to others.
9. We should remember that we are superior to females and not have to depend on them.
10. We should never allow ourselves to be weak or to act like a girl.

This is hardly the formula for a happy, well-balanced life. It's more like a prescription for raising effective workers and warriors, not fathers and husbands and good friends. An important purpose of this book is to help men learn how these beliefs influence our lives, how they damage our personal happiness and the welfare of our families, and how we can challenge these assumptions.

Most of the men I see in my practice have been quite successful at following these rules. In fact one could say that they have been too successful at it. They tend to be well educated and gainfully employed, often in highly respected and lucrative careers. They have provided well for their families. In short, they have pursued the male American dream and seem to have emerged as winners.

Yet for so many men, something doesn't set right. Somewhere in midlife their dream begins to fall apart with some sort of crisis. For one man the turning point came when he started an affair with an employee. For another the crisis came in the form of a heart attack at forty, after seven grueling years of developing his new business. Another man had built a successful medical practice but suddenly detested driving between hospitals. One man became obsessed with hatred for a supervisor who blocked his promotion. Another could not give up his compulsive use of marijuana, despite his wife's threats to leave him if he didn't. Still another could not get his mind off work long enough to get to know his children.

Although their symptoms may have been different, what each of these men had in common was a crisis that exposed their deep sleep.

WHAT IS THE DEEP SLEEP?

Life out of Balance

The primary characteristic of the deep sleep is an unbalanced life. After years of developing the qualities that prepare us for success in the workplace, men often become preoccupied with work and the mind-set it requires. As a result, we have neglected the development of our nurturing, emotional, playful, and creative sides and thus are less effective in places where these traits are needed, particularly in the family.

The workplace becomes more comfortable and rewarding than home. We may spend excessive hours at work and even find ourselves toiling when we're home, by working on the computer, making business phone calls, reading work-related material, or by establishing a home office. Even when not overtly engaged in work-related tasks, men are often preoccupied with thoughts of work. Even when we are busy with our wife or children, part of our mind stays tuned to the work channel. We become emotionally unavailable even when physically present.

The unbalanced man can rationalize the excessive demands of work as necessary and even noble. It is his way of providing for his loved ones. When his wife or children complain that he is too unavailable, he becomes defensive. He fears that if he eases off at work, others will get ahead and achieve the success he so badly needs.

But many men recognize additional reasons for preferring work to home life. One client, an executive working eighty hours a week and more, admitted he liked work more than home because "there I'm the boss, the director. People listen to me, respect me, do what I tell them to do. But when I get home the kids are all over me. They won't give me any space, and they won't do what I tell them to do. And my wife — she often as not ignores me."

Social Isolation

That executive has expressed what many of my clients recognize: They feel isolated from the people around them, especially at home. As a consequence of excessive adherence to the male code, they discover at midlife that the wife and kids are strangers or that they have no close friends.

They might remember fondly the days when they were close to other males, when they could play games, explore their neighborhoods, roll in the snow, or sit around talking for hours until their mothers called them in. During high school they journeyed beyond their neighborhoods in cars, played hockey or basketball together, or gathered late at night in a friend's den to b.s. about their exploits with girls. How sad that most men can't remember making any close friends since their high school or college days.

They might have some good times with the men they meet at work or in the neighborhood, but if one of them changes jobs or moves, they rarely keep in touch, exchanging only an occasional Christmas card. They may write, "Hope to see you soon," but they know the chances are slim.

At midlife, then, many men are socially isolated and confounded as to the cause. They wonder whether it's something personal — a failing or a character flaw. Other men seem to have friends and always seem to have someone to do something with, so why are they alone? Since they rarely talk intimately with others, they have no way of knowing if other men feel socially isolated, too. What may appear to them to be someone's close social network may be as unsatisfying and superficial as their own associations.

The social isolation often extends beyond friends to include family as well. Many men live great distances from their original families, often a result of career relocations.

The contact they do maintain with family and friends tends to be managed by the wife, who frequently serves the function of social manager for their lives. When men marry, they tend to turn over this function to the wife because they consider her more adept at the nuances of social skills. She is the one setting the dates, sending the Christmas cards or party invitations, calling to see how friends are doing.

This social isolation is particularly devastating to a man during a separation or divorce. At his time of greatest need, he finds he has no one to turn to for support. Their mutual friends stay in touch through the wife, and he has not maintained close connections with his family. It's not unusual for a man who has separated to keep it a secret for many weeks or even months.

Mistrusting Our Emotions

Because many men are often unaware of how they feel, they aren't certain about what they truly want. They may be following a track toward career success but are not necessarily excited about the direction the track is leading them in. Often they have become slaves to their jobs. In the pursuit of career goals and in the service of providing for the family, they may have given up creative or artistic endeavors that were important to them in their youth. These have been sacrificed for career goals, logical thinking, and self-discipline.

As men we learn throughout our development that we are supposed to adhere to a strict set of unwritten rules about how to handle and express our emotions. We are cautious about any "excessive" emotional expressiveness lest other men construe it as inappropriate. These rules command us to maintain control of ourselves at all times;

don't let others see how we are feeling; don't be driven by
our emotions but by our rational analytical side; don't feel
sad for ourselves or someone else, because this is a sign of
weakness. For emotional release we play or watch sports or
drink. We show a woman we love her through sex, not by
openly saying what we feel.

These guidelines about emotions and their expression
are taught to men by fathers, peer groups, movies, television, and literature. We look to heroes to provide a model,
but most of these heroes are distant, emotionless men, who
are deemed strong precisely because they do not let their
emotions get in the way. Whether the hero is a basketball
player described as the "ice man" because of his calmness
in the final seconds of a close game, or a president who
doesn't let his fear and compassion block him from
committing troops to a war where many young men and
women might die, he is admired for his ability to control
his emotions. This is not always bad, but it can be extremely
limiting.

As men grow up we discover that keeping our emotions
under control is a formidable task. No matter how hard we
try, feelings always emerge in some form or other. We try
to shut down the source of these strong emotional signals
to keep ourselves from feeling anything.

Likewise we men train ourselves not to be overly sensitive to the feelings of others since they could evoke our
own strong feelings. As boys we learned that empathy was
not valued. To have been described as sensitive or nice was
considered a put-down, even a dangerous challenge to our
manhood. We learned that nice guys finish last. Not until
we are older do we begin to recognize that this axiom is not
necessarily true and that we pay a high price for believing
it is.

The devastating consequences of shutting down our emotional side becomes evident during a crisis. We are supposed to keep a stiff upper lip in the face of loss. But when men experience grief, whether from the loss of a pet, a friendship, or a family member, we fear that somehow our deep pain is a sign of weakness. We face a startlingly powerful conflict: We are supposed to be strong and silent, yet we feel devastated. We therefore conclude that there must be something terribly wrong with us. We not only feel pain but also feel bad about feeling bad. This supposed weakness must be covered up, disguised, or eliminated. This sense that there is something fundamentally wrong with reacting in certain ways is, I believe, at the core of our feelings of shame.

The men I see in my practice who have followed these emotionally restrictive rules for twenty, thirty, or even forty years often appear depressed. They have shut down emotionally. They experience neither intense pain nor intense pleasure. They describe themselves as numb or flat. Depression itself can be defined as the absence of feeling. After many years of trying to control or cover up their feelings, they have succeeded all too well. Yet instead of being proud of their accomplishments, they are like the walking wounded, casualties of a war they were unaware of fighting.

Confusion About Dependency/Intimacy with Women

Perhaps the strongest message men receive has to do with autonomy: "Be your own man," "Don't let anyone push you around," "Don't be a mama's boy." This strongest of messages is also the most confusing. From our earliest years we can remember our fear of being alone. As little children we lived in fear of being separated from our parents. Many men in therapy can recall a common early memory: They are waiting for Dad to come home from work. It's later than usual for his return. The imagination starts running wild. Something has happened to him. How will they be able to take care of themselves without their father?

Herein lies a fundamental paradox of being a man: We know we are supposed to be independent, yet even in adulthood we are plagued by a desire to be taken care of by someone else. When we were young, we looked to our parents for care. Our greatest fear as children was that something would happen to our parents and there would be no one to care for us. We would face the worse situation of all — being abandoned.

In adulthood many men transfer that pattern to their wives or girlfriends. This, too, presents a paradoxical situation. As men we learned to be the dominant sex. The message in its most simple form is "Men are strong, women are weak. A man's job is to protect and take care of the woman in his life." Yet what we are told and what we experience may be two different matters entirely. Our experience tells us that we don't always feel so strong and that many times the woman in our life appears stronger than we do. Especially when it comes to the emotional realm, we may feel inferior to her.

But this is not easy to accept. A man may see his dependence on her as a sign of weakness. After all, he is supposed to be the strong one on whom she can depend. His feelings become confused. Rather than being grateful to his wife for her support, he may tend to downplay the fact, deny it, or, worse, get angry at her for her strength. Men's ridicule of women may be a subconscious attempt to regain the upper hand, to reestablish the dominant position they feel is threatened by allowing themselves to need a woman's help. This pattern of moving between emotional dependency on wives and the reassertion of dominance via anger or ridicule becomes a dangerous, destructive dance men play out in marriage.

This confusion about women has grown even more profound over the past twenty years of the women's movement. The gender men were taught to view as weak and needy has asserted its strength and independence. Men's expectation of a woman waiting to take care of them when they get home has been dashed. Those women, too, are busy making their way in the world.

It is no longer enough for men to go out and make a living. Now many men are expected to pitch in at home, too, doing "women's work," like washing, cooking, and changing diapers. While some may agree intellectually that it is fair for them to help out with these tasks, they struggle with their ingrained beliefs that these duties are unmanly and unimportant — to be done only to placate an angry wife rather than as meaningful tasks on a par with their work outside the home.

This confusion about relationships with women constitutes a fundamental issue for men in the deep sleep. It will be explored in other sections of this book.

Not Taking Care of Ourselves

When we ignore our feelings, we make it more difficult to take good care of ourselves. If we spend our entire lives telling ourselves we are serving others — by working too hard, by worrying too much about earning a living, by being engaged in a competitive orientation to life — we usually have little energy left to take care of ourselves. As men overwork, we feel guilty about relaxing with our families, exercising, or just lying in the hammock. Instead we may eat too much, watch too much TV, or become dependent on alcohol. "It's Miller time" the beer commercial tells us, showing men hard at work on a manly task, then downing a few after their labors. We know these habits are unhealthy, but they are the only means of relaxation we feel comfortable with or find time for. Consequently our health deteriorates.

The sources of this problem are fairly clear. Throughout life the message is to work hard, to be strong and invulnerable. A man imagines himself to be a finely tuned car that is supposed to run without maintenance. "When the going gets tough, the tough get going," Vince Lombardi tells us (from the grave after an early death), and men believe those words. The desire to rest or recreate is a weakness, unless, of course, you have earned a break by your hard work or good deeds.

Many men who enter therapy have faced a crisis brought on by bad health, by trying to stifle the healthy voice that says, "You're working too hard," "You're eating the wrong food," "You haven't exercised in two weeks." This is the forty-year-old with a history of heart disease who fails to get a physical and ends up with a heart attack. Or the thirty-five-year-old self-made businessman who continues to smoke after three hospitalizations for pulmonary infection. Or the fifty-four-year-old diabetic who disbelieves the doctor and neglects his medication.

For many men alcohol and drugs are the only acceptable way to cope with the pressures of being a man. A familiar pattern is coffee (and perhaps cigarettes) to get the engines running in the morning, constant refueling with caffeine throughout the day, followed by alcohol, marijuana, or cocaine in the evening to calm down and relax. The evening intake leads to the morning sluggishness, which is corrected by the caffeine, and on it goes. Many men follow this pattern for years without recognizing the deleterious effects on their systems. Only when someone (usually the wife) complains about the effects of the substances does this pattern become an issue to consider.

Substance abuse is one of the major contributors to the deep sleep. Alcohol and marijuana reinforce habits of passivity and inactivity. The use of substances may also be an attempt at self-medication. Alcohol and tobacco are available, acceptable, and affordable, and they promise to ease stress, discomfort, or pain. But in due time rather than having any medicinal effect, they become the source of new pain. They become addictions. (The complex relationship between substance abuse and masculinity is a topic that we will explore in more detail in chapter 4.)

Another detriment to men's health is our tendency to speed up our lives. Faced with the mandate to be successful at all endeavors, and living in a time of rapid social change, men have responded by trying to go faster. Being an effective time manager has become a new, subtle form of being the master of our own fate. If we could just go faster, work smarter, be more efficient, be better organized, the theory goes, we could be more successful and therefore more satisfied.

Logan Wright, a psychologist, has studied the relationship between Type A behavior (the driven, compulsive, workaholic personality) and coronary heart disease. He finds that the most dangerous element of the Type A pattern of personality is this sense of living a speeded-up life-style. He identifies three central ingredients of this pattern: a sense of time urgency (trying to make every second count); chronic activation ("a tendency to stay active or keyed up most of the day, every day"); and being "multiphasic" ("a tendency both to have many irons in the fire and to do more than one thing at a time"). He finds that men who follow this pattern significantly raise their risk of developing coronary heart disease. (See "Type A Behavioral Patterns and Coronary Artery Disease," *American Psychologist* 43, 1 [January, 1988]: 2–14.)

I believe this pattern may be a direct outgrowth of the male dictate to tend to those parts of self that help achieve success and to ignore those parts that may detract from the pursuit. Men in the deep sleep routinely report that getting the most out of their time is a top priority. They describe their lives with words such as *hectic, busy, rushed.* Rarely do they know how to take life easy or to slow down.

Another aspect of not taking good care of ourselves is shutting down our playful, creative sides. Men have let activities we loved as kids fall by the wayside. I loved to play hockey as a boy, but now I rarely find the time to lace up my skates. When one client, Derrick, became a dentist, his love of the saxophone was shelved. Rick put off sculpting when he began his work at the real estate agency and never got back to it. The pattern is pervasive. Most men have sacrificed their athletic or artistic interests to pursue careers that promised greater financial rewards and prestige.

The fast-track life-style can also leave us with unhealthy sexual lives. I see two categories of sexual dysfunction among men in my practice. The first consists of men who find sex one of their only satisfying outlets and become obsessed with it. In the second category are men who find themselves losing interest in sex and who are worried about the cause of their apathy. Both patterns can lead to serious trouble: strained relationships with one's wife or girlfriend; affairs; the development of forms of sexual addiction; depression and severe self-doubt. Although men usually do not seek out counseling primarily for a sexual problem, it is quite common for them to express some confusion and doubt about their sexuality when they become comfortable with the therapist.

AWAKENING FROM THE DEEP SLEEP

How do men begin the process of awakening from the deep sleep? The fact that you're reading this book indicates that the process has already begun. Whether you picked up this book based on the recommendation of a friend, at the insistence of a loved one, out of a state of discomfort that drove you to the self-help section of your bookstore, or just out of curiosity, the act of reading a book about men and change suggests that you have begun to explore masculine conditioning and its effects on you. You have already received your wake-up call. This curiosity is the most crucial beginning step of the journey.

As soon as you begin to question the rules and regulations of masculine conditioning, you have crossed an important barrier. You have begun to recognize masculinity for what it is: a social construct whose rules, mores, and conventions are established by society. It is no longer etched in stone, an immutable given that cannot be questioned, challenged, or changed. For you the journey toward awakening has already begun.

For many the beginning of the journey is not pleasant. In fact some may have come to this juncture out of one of the most painful experiences of their lives. The journey began for some with a crisis, seemingly initiated by someone else. The awakening may have begun abruptly, the man startled awake by his wife's announcement that if he didn't change, she would leave. He may have had some vague awareness that things were not great in the marriage, and he may even have tried to change his patterns; but the threat to leave (or the actual leaving) came as a complete surprise. It probably sent him into a panic, which woke him up as if a loud explosion had gone off. For others the awakening may have been triggered by a boss who blocked a promotion or by the loss of a friend, acquaintance, or even the death of a dear pet.

Whatever the cause, the reactions are much the same: a sense of confusion; a questioning of long-held values; a sense of desperation — that something must change or else; an unprecedented sense of panic. He may feel like a kid whose scary-faced jack-in-the-box has popped up and refuses to be stuffed back in.

Because you are a man who has strived to live by the rules of manhood, you probably are alone in your moment of crisis. If you are like most men, you have been socially isolated, with nowhere to turn at this dark time. If you usually seek your wife's support and she is the one you are at odds with, you can hardly turn to her. You may think of calling on a male friend, but your feelings of pride get in the way. "What would he think?" "He wouldn't have the time to help." "He'd only give advice." "He might not keep a confidence."

Perhaps you think of calling on a family member, but here, too, lies danger. You may have tried for many years to keep your distance from your parents in order to maintain a hard-won sense of independence. If you admit vulnerability to them, you may open the floodgates to a torrent of advice on how you should live your life. Or perhaps you hesitate to contact parents or siblings because they have their own problems. You wouldn't want to burden them with your issues.

At a time of crisis, therefore, you may find yourself alone, bewildered, and with nowhere to turn. I hope this book will fill that void.

WHAT TO EXPECT

This book is designed to help men recognize, alter, and if possible prevent the patterns of the deep sleep. My task is threefold: first, in this and in the next two chapters to help the reader understand what the deep sleep is and how we have tended to fall into it; second, to offer guidelines for developing a fuller, more balanced life; and third, in chapters 4 through 8, to suggest ways to stay out of the deep sleep and to work to change patterns so that others, including and most importantly our children, will not follow the same script.

Throughout the book I use the stories of the men I have worked with over the years to show how they have been able to awaken from the deep sleep. I follow several men as they go through the process of awakening so you can have positive models for negotiating the necessary changes.

I draw on techniques for change that I have learned from professional publications and discussions during my career as a psychologist. I also draw on my own experiences as a man in midlife who, like you, has been struggling to understand what it means to be a man as we approach the twenty-first century.

By the end of this book I hope you will have learned the following insights and skills to carry you through the challenges you face in midlife.

- To understand and acknowledge how you feel and to know better what you truly want in your life.

- To recognize the sources of your anger that stem from male conditioning and how to avoid dominating and overpowering others.

- To understand your beliefs about yourself and how they affect your attitudes and behavior toward women and children.

- To assess how you have been affected by the so-called sexual revolution.

- To better understand your family of origin and how to deal more effectively with and less reactively to your parents (living or dead) and siblings.

- To overcome your social isolation and reconnect with old friends and make new ones.

- To rediscover creative and loving parts of yourself that have lain dormant or hidden due to your excessive adherence to the "virility code." Most important among these are the parts of you that enable you to love yourself — as a man and as a human being.

- To begin to restore balance to your life so that you are not overwhelmed by the demands of your job or the excessive demands you place on yourself.

I realize this is a lot to learn. I will be inviting you to take risks in ways that may be more threatening (and exciting) than driving a motorcycle at breakneck speed. These are interpersonal risks that will challenge many of the rules you learned about how you should act, think, and feel as a man.

What are the risks? What are the challenges you face as a man in midlife?

FIVE CHALLENGES FOR MEN AT MIDLIFE

1. Learning to trust your emotions and to rediscover your creative side.

2. Renegotiating and revitalizing your relationship with women and children.

3. Reevaluating your sexuality.

4. Redefining your relationship with your family of origin.

5. Learning to (re)connect with other men.

In the remainder of this book you will discover how you came to be this way, and you will learn what you can do to meet these five challenges successfully.

2 UNDERSTANDING THE CAUSES OF THE DEEP SLEEP

Scott was clearly hurting. As the group started he was eager to talk about his problem. At age forty-two he had been separated for two months from his wife of twenty years. During most of that time he had been faithful to her, except for a few times when he had "strayed," as he put it. Now she had found out about it and was threatening to file for divorce. He was in a panic. The thought of losing her and his three young children was more than he could bear. With the impact of the crisis hitting him full force, he was now finally beginning to understand the seriousness of his problem: being inattentive to his wife and fantasizing about having sex with every attractive woman he saw. Usually he could resist, but not always. Now he realized he needed his wife desperately and could not imagine life without her and his children.

As he talked to the group about the nature of his problem, he asked me two important questions: What caused his problem, and what were the solutions to it? I was jolted by the directness and simplicity of these questions. Part of me was relieved that Scott, with whom I had struggled in the group for over a year, was finally beginning to comprehend the dimensions of his problem. Yet I was anxious: How could I begin to explain to him what had caused his problem? He was so earnest in wanting to know, but I was aware that the answer to his question was complicated. So, too, with the solutions. No single action or insight was going to solve his problem, just as no single factor had caused it. By the end of that tumultuous group session, Scott was beginning to understand the causes of his problems and seemed eager to continue to search for their solutions. What Scott began in the group that day is similar to what I hope to be able to help the reader do in this book.

When we hear that one of our friends has a problem, our first impulse is usually to search for the immediate causes in the person's life. If a man suddenly leaves his wife for another woman, for example, we look for direct explanations: "He left because their sex life was lousy" or "He was drinking too much and it impaired his judgment" or "He was seduced by that pretty woman who was after his money."

After the initial shock wears off, we might widen our lens to search for solutions that have more to do with his particular history or with the history of the relationship: "He never got over the death of his father when he was a young boy" or "He couldn't cope when his wife went back to work and became more successful than he was."

A few of his friends may even offer more global explanations of his behavior: "With the pressures on men these days to stay young, it's no wonder he found a younger woman" or "The way we're raised to view women as sex objects, it's not surprising that he succumbed to the expectation." As a psychologist I could argue with any of these explanations, yet each offers a partial explanation for disturbing behavior (at least it's disturbing to those who are trying to maintain a marriage).

The lens analogy enables us to understand the link between a set of explanations at one level and another. The narrow focus gives us a close-up view of the situation, providing enough detail for us to gain an individual psychological understanding of the problem. As we widen the lens we see the individual man in a wider context of the systems in which he operates: first the family; then the work system; next the community; then the society. To understand behavior fully we need to draw on explanations from each of these contexts.

FAMILY SYSTEMS CABLE: A FRAMEWORK FOR UNDERSTANDING

For Scott to begin to see how his particular problems developed, he needed a framework or scheme to be able to understand himself. As a family therapist, the particular framework I use is called the *Family Systems Perspective*. With this framework we seek an understanding of an individual through the connections among the various social systems that influence a person's life in the past, present, and future.

Lynn Hoffman, a social worker and family therapy theoretician, has developed a useful metaphor for understanding how systems influence an individual. In this metaphor she asks us to imagine an individual as embedded in the center of a cable (see fig. 1). The individual is a system unto himself or herself, which in turn is composed of various subsystems, such as the digestive, reproductive, and circulatory systems ("A Co-Evolutionary Framework

Figure 1. Family Systems Cable

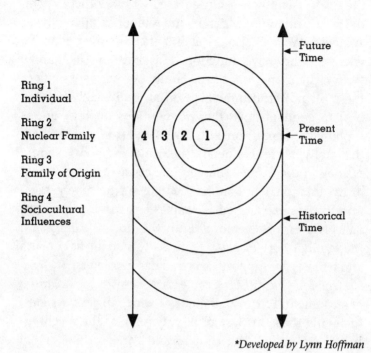

Ring 1
Individual

Ring 2
Nuclear Family

Ring 3
Family of Origin

Ring 4
Sociocultural
Influences

Future
Time

Present
Time

Historical
Time

Developed by Lynn Hoffman

for Systemic Family Therapy," in *Diagnosis: Assessment in Family Therapy,* ed. J. Hansen [Rockville, MA: Aspen Publishers, 1983], 35–59).

Perhaps the most complex and certainly most relevant to us is the central nervous system, which directs our thinking, feeling, and behavior. How the individual acts is in turn related to the other layers of the cable. In the second ring is the nuclear family, which is responsible for many important functions, including teaching the individual, providing nurturance and shelter for its members, and passing on family traditions. In ring three we see that the nuclear family is again encased with another system: the family of origin, which includes blood relatives, living and dead. We may also think of it encompassing adoptive relatives who have functioned as part of the family. Within the framework of the family of origin are some of the most powerful influences on an individual: rules on how to conduct one's life; prescriptions on how one is supposed to express oneself; myths and stories about how the family has functioned in the world and how it should operate in the future. These influences may be functional or dysfunctional and are handed down from one generation to the next through examples of behavior, story, ritual, pictures, or ceremony. Both the nuclear family and the family of origin have definite ideas about how males and females are supposed to conduct themselves.

The fourth ring of the cable is the family's sociocultural environment. This ring includes a wide range of systems, including those in close proximity, such as the neighborhood, the school, the church; and those farther out in ever-widening circles, including work systems, city, state, and national political systems, religion, and economics.

Although each of these systems can be viewed as having an impact on the individual, from a systems perspective the influence is interactive. The individual also influences the systems.

In addition to space, the cable has another dimension: time. When we look at an individual, such as Scott, we see him at only one point in time. But Scott and the various systems in which he lives have a history. Scott has lived through the Vietnam War, which had a powerful impact on all young men at the time, whether they went into the service or found a way to avoid the draft. Men now in midlife have also experienced two tremendously important social movements: the civil rights movement and the women's movement.

When we expand outward in the cable, we take into account two powerful historical events in our parents' lives: the Great Depression of 1929 and World War II. Many of our beliefs and attitudes today have their roots in our family's response to these events. My grandfather, for example, had been well off before the Depression but then fell into poverty after the crash. To try to regain his former status, he began to gamble and developed a destructive habit that plagued him for his entire life. It eventually caused him to become depressed and to take his own life. The impact of his suicide on me was probably an important factor in my selecting psychology as a career.

An interesting dimension of the cable is that it extends into the future as well as the past. This means that how we project ourselves into the future also influences how we act in the present. Dick presented an interesting example of the impact of future thinking. He revealed that he was planning to give up his job at the age of fifty because he believed he was only going to live to fifty-six. When asked why, he said that his father had died of heart disease at fifty-six, and he believed that he had only six years to live and didn't want to spend them in the office. He had worked like a dog for the past twenty years to be able to have enough money to spend his last six years having some fun. Here is a fascinating example of how the past, present, and future can be interactive. Interestingly, Dick had never gone to the doctor to see how his heart was functioning.

THE SOCIOCULTURAL RING

In our search to understand how the deep sleep pattern develops in men, we begin by focusing on the fourth and outermost ring in the cable, the sociocultural context.

A universal view of the male species seems to exist that holds that in society the male has three primary roles: provider, protector, and impregnator. This view was upheld in a recent important and influential ethnographic study by the anthropologist David Gilmore, in which he asked the question, Does there exist a code of manliness that is consistent around the world? After studying a variety of men, including hunters, fishermen, workers, warriors, poets, and peasants, from several diverse cultures he concluded that the view of man as "protector, provider, and impregnator" was indeed universal (with a few notable exceptions).

Furthermore, Gilmore noted that for men to play out these roles, there exists a universal expectation that men must be "tough, aggressive, stoic, and (hetero)sexual." Throughout the world through the trials of initiation, a young man is pressured by his elders to act tough and fearless.

Gilmore also found that from culture to culture a man's life is an ongoing series of tests that must be passed in the public arena to continually prove his manhood. It is not enough to pass through puberty; a male must face a continuing series of challenges to his manhood. If he backs down, he risks losing his designation as "a real man" and is instead viewed by society as something less than a man, someone to be scorned and rejected.

Raised to Work

In the 1990s the mandate for men to be providers has translated into the male preoccupation with work and career. In my first book, *Men in Therapy: The Challenge of Change*, I described modern men as being "raised to work." For most men work is central, the place where we define who we are, establish our feelings of self-worth, and strive for the money necessary to attain our desired lifestyle. By working we feel responsible as men, that somehow through providing financially for the family we are fulfilling our primary responsibility. When men are deprived of the opportunity to work — whether because of unemployment or illness — we feel diminished as men. Our self-esteem takes a battering, and we look to other, often destructive, outlets as ways to feel good about ourselves as men.

The focus on "men as workers" is related to the excessive focus on competitiveness among men. Work takes place in a competitive, hierarchical structure in the capitalist economy. As we grow up male, we constantly receive messages about winning at all costs (competing against others) and working to our fullest potential (competing against ourselves). This is reflected in the nature of the social systems that are designed to rear boys and girls. The school system, for example, is usually structured on a basis of competition. Even from the early years, children are graded, which emphasizes comparisons between children and inevitably leads to competition. If a child is not bright or is learning disabled, this process of comparison can lead to deep feelings of shame. Ed, now age forty, was a poor student in elementary school. He bitterly recalls the shame of report card days. He would leave school quickly and run to hide in an empty field so other children or his parents would not ask about his grades.

Sports programs, so crucial to most young boys, are likewise highly competitive. Games are won or lost, batting averages are calculated, team standings are determined. By the age of ten many boys participate in the daily male ritual of reading the sports pages, which are rife with statistics, box scores, standings, game results, and players' salaries. At an early age a boy who is not a "good enough" athlete will be cut from a team. John, who loved baseball, recalls watching from behind a grove of trees as his friends played on the junior high school baseball team. He had been afraid to go out for the team lest he be embarrassed by not making it. At age thirteen his dream of a baseball career was over and his sense of inferiority had begun.

This obsession with keeping score overflows from school and the team into social interactions. Boys learn from an early age to compare themselves with other boys (and girls) on a variety of levels: who is bigger; stronger; faster; smarter; funnier; braver; better looking; who lives in a bigger house; whose father drives a sportier car; whose mother is prettier; who is more popular. The focus on comparison or keeping score can become an obsession, but it is not just a mental exercise. It can have real consequences for boys: who makes the team; who is in the top band; who dates the prettiest girl; who is in the advanced placement courses in high school — all of these comparative statistics can determine how a boy perceives himself and how he measures up in a world where competition can have a profound impact on his access to power and achievement.

Raised to War

In our society, a man is also supposed to be the protector of society and the family. I recall watching the television coverage of a young man leaving for Saudi Arabia from his air force base in the Upper Peninsula of Michigan shortly before Christmas 1990. The reporter asked him how he was feeling about going off to war. Without a moment's hesitation, he said he was looking forward to it: "This is what I've been training for, and now the opportunity's here and I can't wait to get into it."

He was referring specifically to the training he received in the air force, but in many subtle ways the socialization he experienced growing up for twenty years had been preparing him for this moment. We learn socio-cultural norms about how to behave as men that are quite adaptable to the role of soldier. Let us examine some of these messages.

It is not acceptable for males to admit to physical pain or fear. The adage "Big boys don't cry" is no joke. We take it quite seriously from the time we are young. We learn that we are supposed to tolerate physical pain or discomfort without flinching or crying. We learn that we are supposed to "take it like a man," which means no expression that it hurts. If we complain, we are ridiculed: "What's the matter, can't you take it?" "Don't be a wimp." One man recalls having his thumb smashed when a foul tip hit him while playing catcher. As his father took him for X rays, he remembers praying that his thumb was broken so that he wouldn't be criticized for complaining so vehemently about a mere sprain. A cast would have been his badge of courage.

To express fear is shameful, especially if it is fear of another boy. Mike recalls being bullied in his neighborhood by Harvey, another boy who was the same age and about the same size. The only difference between them as far as Mike could figure was that Harvey didn't seem to fear pain and Mike did. As a result, Harvey would push Mike around, take food and money from him, and even make Mike go to the store for him. What kept Mike immobilized was his fear of being beaten up by Harvey, who bragged of being in training for the Golden Gloves boxing tournament. Harvey didn't seem afraid of being hit, but Mike was terrified of it. Forty years later when Mike recounted this story in therapy, he became so emotionally charged that he admitted he still thought about going back to his hometown and beating the crap out of Harvey.

Males must conform to the norms of the peer group. The pressure to conform to the male norms is powerful, even if the norms are at variance with those of the family. One mandate of the adolescent peer culture is Don't back down from a challenge. We can see how this mandate is excellent training for the role of soldier, which requires fearlessness. But the consequences for a young boy trying to adapt to this mandate without adequate understanding of it can be devastating.

Rick, for example, recalls the time he first received his driver's license and was given his parents' car to go to a football game. After the game he and his friends got into a shouting match with some boys from the opposing school. The boys challenged them to a fight out in the country. Rick did not want to go. He knew he would get into trouble with his parents and he feared getting into a fight. But he feared worse the scorn of his peers if he backed down from the challenge. Driving fast through the countryside, he failed to see a car off the side of the road, and he struck the driver, who was trying to flag him down.

Rick's story illustrates the fierce power the male peer group wields in the life of a boy growing up in our culture. Conformity to the group is paramount, even if this means defying the family's teachings and facing distinct dangers.

The peer group has supplanted adult males in the process of initiating boys into manhood. Preoccupied with the pursuit of their careers, adult men are not available to provide leadership or to direct rites of passage for boys. Out of this void comes an excessive reliance on the peer group to provide the rites of passage. It is a case of the young leading the younger, or the blind leading the blind. This pattern is extremely pronounced in the parts of our culture where males tend to be absent altogether from the family and even from the community. Sociologists link the powerful influence of gangs on inner-city youth and the absence of adult males in inner-city families. Without adult male role models to look up to, boys look to other boys to provide examples of how to live.

Derrick, who grew up without a father, recalls being initiated into manhood through membership in a Detroit street gang. Although he did not feel comfortable with the expectations of the group, he felt that he had no alternatives. "It was either be part of the group — dress as they did, go where they went — or else stay inside the apartment afraid to go out on the street and be hassled by the other gangs."

The power of the peer group does not stop with high school. Each fall and spring we witness a rite of passage on college campuses as men are initiated into fraternities. Fraternity hazing eerily imitates military boot camp, which is a sanctified rite of passage in American society. The pledges are made to feel inferior to the frat elders, who put them through a series of humiliating public activities, often forcing them to drink excessively and to exercise to the point of exhaustion.

The degradation of women is also part of the fraternity initiation rites. The "plebes" who are put in a one-down position by their "older brothers" often in turn gather in groups to put women in a one-down position to themselves. In an article on sexual harassment, the *Utne Reader* (May/June 1990) reported incidents on college campuses that included young men whistling and shouting obscenities at women as they walked by fraternity houses and routinely harassing women who supported women's rights. In one incident a group of men yelled obscenities and threw beer at women rallying against date rape on campus.

Another aspect of the sociocultural influence on males is homophobia. We are taught to hate homosexuals. Since it is common for most boys to have some homosexual feelings while growing up, this message of hatred strikes terror into all males. If homosexuals are to be hated and derided, but we experience homosexual feelings from time to time, does this mean that if we reveal our feelings we ourselves will be hated and derided? The confusion is made even more profound because boys are taught to fear homosexuals even before they have a rudimentary understanding of sexuality.

This confusion spawns the notion that somehow homosexuals are men who act like women. Therefore to avoid the possibility of being categorized as homosexual, boys go out of their way to avoid anything that may appear feminine. Boys learn that any activity not clearly masculine should be avoided. This becomes very confusing for boys who are interested in the arts. In Western society most of the arts, except perhaps rock music, have come to be seen as feminine. By the age of ten or eleven, consequently, many boys who enjoy playing the piano or violin want to give it up. It is not valued by their male peers, who emphasize more daring or competitive activities. To continue to play classical piano (jazz or rock may be OK) is to risk being deemed unmanly.

Because most boys have not been taught about sexuality by their parents, they turn to the peer group for information. Of course a fourteen-year-old cannot explain to a twelve-year-old the subtleties of sexual fantasy. So when the twelve-year-old experiences a sexual feeling for another boy, or perhaps, quite commonly, has a sexual encounter with another boy, he goes into a homosexual panic, fearing that he may be gay. In reaction he may try to become ultramacho, demonstrating to himself and to his male peer group how "manly" he really is.

For many men the homosexual fear continues into adulthood. Roger, a forty-six-year-old pilot, revealed to me that he experienced impotence after his divorce. He feared that his failure sexually might mean that he was homosexual. Our conversations disclosed no indications that he had any sexual interest in men, but he had learned to equate sex with performance and achievement. He thought it was his job to perform sexually. If he failed sexually, he was not a man. If he was not a man, so the logic went, he was secretly homosexual.

The United States military is an extremely homophobic system. Any member of the military, male or female, found to be homosexual is immediately discharged. Why is the military so intolerant of homosexuality? Do they think that for people to be effective soldiers they must adhere strictly to the norms of gender-role conditioning?

As I write about homophobia, I recognize the importance of examining my own attitudes toward homosexual men. Even though I have been a therapist for almost twenty years and have worked with many men who have struggled with the issue of sexual preference, I recognize that homophobia is still partially embedded in my own consciousness, as I believe it is in most men's. Given the pervasiveness of homophobia in our country, it is no surprise that homosexuality remains a taboo topic for most straight men. If it comes up in conversation between men, it is usually in a context of derision or scandal. Yet for these same men the avoidance of appearing "unmanly" is a major motivation behind much of their behavior — how they dress, how they talk, how they walk, what their interests are. Why is appearing manly so important? What are they afraid of? We will return to this important topic in chapter 6, on sexuality.

Man as Procreator

Now we turn to the third dimension of Gilmore's description of the male role, man as procreator or impregnator. Of the three roles Gilmore outlines, that of procreator is suffering perhaps the most ambiguity among men and women in 1990s. On a basic level, significant technological changes have altered the traditional assumption that men are necessary for impregnation. With artificial insemination it is now possible for a woman to become pregnant without having sexual intercourse with a man. Through artificial insemination, a few men can provide enough sperm to impregnate all of the women who desire children for years to come. Furthermore, through a second technological innovation, the vasectomy, several million men have opted to stop impregnating women.

Other sociocultural changes have also altered the role of man as creator of children. In many societies the importance of fathering children seems to vary with social class. Those men on the lower economic rungs seem to place a higher value on procreation than those who are more affluent. Poorer men may use the number of children fathered as one way to keep score of their manhood. If he cannot score big financially due to the social and educational disadvantages he faces, then a man can prove his virility through procreation. Males (many of them in their teens) pressure females to have sex and consider it as unmanly to use birth control. Making a female pregnant is viewed as a sign of virility among male peers and accords a man status. This pattern, related more to socioeconomic status than race, deserves more attention in the research on the teenage pregnancy problem.

At the other end of the economic ladder, more affluent males have become so focused on education, career, and making money that they hesitate to commit to a relationship at all. When they do, they are often reluctant to have children. Many fear that parenting responsibilities would interfere with their pursuit of career success.

This does not mean that men in this economic class do not want to have sex. They simply are less likely to want a woman to become pregnant. In fact if we include having sex with women as part of the definition of procreator, then this aspect of the gender role is a tremendously important motivating factor for most men.

Most men view having sex with women as the ultimate achievement and the consummate source of pleasure. This almost goes without saying. Sex is the prominent topic of television, movies, newspapers, and magazines. It is the favorite material of comedians. From the time an adolescent boy understands rudimentary sex, his thoughts turn constantly in that direction, and his mind is full of fantasies of having sex with a variety of women.

For many men the thoughts become an obsession. They cannot look at a woman without evaluating her as a potential sex partner and gauging their chances of getting her into bed. Regardless of class, men talk to one another about women in sexual terms. Two stories I heard recently illustrate this point.

Scott, a lawyer in a prestigious firm, went out to dinner with a group of lawyers and businessmen. A married lawyer in his fifties who happened to be sitting next to Scott made lewd sexual comments about several women who passed by — "Look at those legs," "What a pair she has," "I'd love to get her in the sack." He made these suggestions not quietly but loudly enough for everyone at the table to hear. No one tried to quiet him, no one registered any discomfort. For the men it was de rigueur, like a familiar and humorous ritual.

Rick, a real estate broker, was questioning my assertion that he might be sexually addicted. "I'm no different from all the men I work with," he said. "At lunch yesterday one of the guys asked us what we would do if Jill, a young woman in the office, went out to her van in the parking lot, took off all her clothes, rolled down the window and invited us in? Would any of you guys — married or not, religious or not — be able to resist? Not for a minute. Every man said he'd be in that van in a second and be willing to do anything she asked of him."

Rick looked at me cooly. "If I'm a sex addict, so are all the guys I work with." I could argue with Rick, but he did have a point. We were reared in a culture dominated by the model of men as sexual conquistadors. Although some of us may have been raised in a religious atmosphere, the most prevailing philosophy was the playboy philosophy. Our early gurus were men like Hugh Hefner and Henry Miller. Our bibles were *Playboy, Penthouse,* or their predecessors, such as *Argosy.* The comedian we really wanted to hear was Lenny Bruce, not Jerry Lewis. Our idea of a real woman was Marilyn Monroe or Sophia Loren. June Cleaver on "Leave It to Beaver" was fine as a mother; but in our youth we weren't interested in finding a wife. We wanted sex. Being a virgin was not really being a man. Losing our virginity became an obsession, as if virginity was a plague that had to be cured before we could pass into manhood. From this perspective, females were mere means to an end. They were not real persons; they were ways for us to lose our virginity.

Yet despite their tough talk, many men fell in love in the process of pursuing sex, and that combined experience of sex and love set off an emotional earthquake that was more powerful than anything they had ever experienced before (and some wonder whether they'll ever experience it again). After years of growing up with the goal of trying to control their emotions, suddenly their emotions and libido burst forth upon their unsuspecting minds with great intensity. If they thought hitting a home run or scoring a goal on a breakaway was a thrill, this was in a class of ecstasy by itself. It was an experience that would alter their lives in unimaginable ways.

Unfortunately many men were unprepared to deal with it. Unaccustomed to living in an emotional world, they found love to be like experiencing the wonder of scuba diving without the right equipment. It was great until they had to take the next breath. Suddenly strong men became childlike in the arms of a woman. A man who was so crafty at seducing a woman found himself dependent on her. He had planned to lose his virginity but his independence was another matter.

Dean, a star hockey and baseball player in high school, recalled falling in love at age seventeen with Bonnie. At first he thought he was doing her a favor. She was not very popular, but she was pretty, and he thought he could easily "score" with her. After a few dates they were becoming quite sexual, but Dean surprised himself by starting to have feelings for her. "At first I didn't know what was going on," he recalled twenty-five years later. "I had been used to acting hard, never showing my feelings to anyone. Suddenly I couldn't get her off my mind. I couldn't stand to be away from her; couldn't stand to see her around any other guys. I didn't know whether it was love or lust or both, but I knew she was driving me crazy."

And indeed Dean didn't know what to do with the feelings. He tried treating Bonnie mean, as he had seen in the movies. He flirted with other women, bossed her around, played hard to get. Yet when she would go out with another guy, he felt like he was going out of his mind. He loved how he felt when he was with her, yet he hated her for making him depend on her.

Dean and Bonnie came to see me twenty-five years later for marital therapy. Dean was still experiencing the same emotional push/pull, the same closeness/distance dance that he had begun with Bonnie when both were teenagers. In a surprising way much remained the same in those twenty-five years, but much had changed in their relationship, too. Perhaps the biggest change had been not in Dean but in Bonnie. From 1968 to 1988, she had felt the impact of the women's movement in the United States. From a seventeen-year-old girl whose biggest goal had been to "get" the school's BMOC, she was now her own person. At age forty-two, she was in a Ph.D. program in nursing. In a few years she would be able to earn sixty thousand dollars a year. But that would require moving. Could Dean, who had been used to calling the shots in their marriage, handle moving for his wife's career? Could he imagine a commuter marriage? Could he imagine putting his law career on hold to spend more time at home with their three children? Could he learn to understand how his sudden interest in other women was related to Bonnie's return to school?

Dean and Bonnie's dilemma underscores perhaps the most significant sociocultural phenomenon for men at midlife. The women's movement (most men are not even sure what to call it—the women's lib movement, the feminist movement, women's lib, or the radical feminist movement?) has had a powerful impact on us in ways we could not have imagined when it began twenty years ago. Many men laughed at the bra-burners (I wonder whether a man or a woman made up that term), and some believed that those "pushy women" were just trying to steal the thunder from the civil rights movement (I remember saying that myself when I was a graduate student in 1970).

But as I look at my own life and the lives of my male clients today, I believe that the women's movement has altered our lives in ways we are just beginning to realize. Furthermore I believe that within that movement lie the seeds of our own liberation as men. What we do with it is the crucial question for our era. We may try to squelch it — to ridicule it, to scorn it, to pay it only lip service — or we may try to understand it and embrace it. Whatever way we choose, the women's movement is the key point where we stand now on the sociocultural time cable. We will explore its implications further in subsequent chapters. But first we move to chapter 3 to look at men in the context of family.

3 A FRAMEWORK FOR UNDERSTANDING OUR FAMILIES

The men were in a somber mood as the group began. Phil had missed the last group to attend his father's funeral in Nebraska. When Phil walked in this evening, the others acknowledged him with warm and understanding looks. They were uncertain what to say. Finally Mike broke the awkward silence, "Sorry to hear about your father," he said. Thankful that Mike had started, the others followed suit — virtually the same words, the same looks, the same absence of touch.

They listened respectfully as Phil described receiving the dreaded call from his stepmother. "Your father died peacefully in his sleep," she related. "Apparently it was a heart attack. He suffered no pain." Phil explained to the group that his father had hoped to die this way. At age seventy-eight, having had two previous heart attacks, he knew the end was near even though he had been healthy and happy for the past few years. "Even in his death, dad lived by a plan," Phil said. "His entire life he did everything according to a plan. His papers were in perfect order, everything was arranged to make it easy for us kids."

After describing the details of the funeral, Phil flashed back four months to Christmastime, when at the group's urging he had paid a visit to his father with the intent of trying to get closer to this meticulous, overly controlled man, who had been Phil's only parent since his mother died when Phil was a teenager. Phil had been bitter toward his father since then, especially resentful of the manner in which his father had forced the family to handle his mom's death. It was a matter of taking care of business, of details — the burial, the disposing of her "things." There was no room for grieving. "No emotion allowed" was how Phil described it. Phil was left alone with his pain. The only indication he had that his father was hurting, too, was when he would see the red flicker of his father's cigarette as he sat on the porch late at night with a drink in his hand, in the dead of the Nebraska winter.

Phil thanked the group for having urged him to go back that previous Christmas. He had traveled with the idea that he would "really try to talk to his father," really try to break through his father's superficiality and stiffness. He wanted to learn from his father what he really thought about him, whether his father really approved of his career choice, or whether he looked down on him because a degree in education was not manly enough, not as good as his father's career as a dentist. Although the visit was pleasant enough, Phil had not gotten what he wanted from his father. His father could make small talk, but he could not talk at the emotional level that Phil desired. But during that visit he had managed to talk at that level with his siblings and realized that they felt much the same way about their father as he did. They, too, felt something was missing in their relationship with him.

Somehow out of that trip and the talk with his siblings Phil felt like he had come to a resolution with his father. He had begun to realize that the things he wanted from his father were never going to come. His father wasn't going to change, and it was no use for him continually to try to win his father's approval. He stopped blaming his father. He began to forgive him. By recognizing his father's limitations, he could begin to appreciate his father for who he was, and he could give up blaming him for not being the father Phil wished he would be.

"I just wish I could have told him this," Phil went on, now almost in tears, "how much he meant to me, what a powerful presence in my life he had been; it was not always a good presence — at times it was almost over-whelming — but I loved him and I miss him terribly."

The others sat listening to Phil in stunned silence. I knew the next question that had to be asked. It was the one most on my mind as I thought of my own seventy-five-year-old father: "How would each of you react if you received a call like Phil's?"

Mike said it would trigger "major sadness. My own father had to make the decision to take his father off life-support systems. I would never want to be in that position. I have trouble talking to my father, too. The only time I remember crying in front of him was when he took me to see *Old Yeller*. That was one of the most special moments of my life. But as I got older, whenever I started to cry he would say, 'If you're thinking about crying, I'll give you something to cry about.'"

Arnie said he'd been thinking about sending his father a letter. "I've been feeling closer to dad since I went on that trip with him last summer. I drove him to his home-town, and we spent the day going places together. We drove past the farm where he was raised, and we ate at the old hotel in town. We also visited the graves of his par-ents, my grandparents. That trip was very special. It drew us a lot closer, but I haven't talked much to him lately.

He's not much of a phone talker, he just gives me over to Mom. Maybe a letter letting him know how special that trip was would be just the right thing for me."

Tom was uncertain how he would feel if anything happened to his dad. He had made numerous attempts to spend some one-to-one time with his father, who was a drinking alcoholic when Tom was growing up. He had stopped drinking many years ago due to serious health problems, but Tom still found him unapproachable. "Besides, I can never get him away from my mother. They are inseparable, and she's the talker. When they're together he takes a backseat and doesn't say much. Yet they're together all the time. I want to keep trying to get close to the old guy, but I'm not sure I'll ever be able to."

Scott, too, at the urging of the group had tried to talk to his father a few months earlier during a trip to Florida. But he found his father irritable, angry, and annoying, just as he had been all of his life. "My father has not had a very happy life. He's miserable now and has been for most of his life. He believes in heaven, and I think death will be a relief for him. He's sixty-four but looks ninety-four. My brothers told me not to stir things up with dad. I don't know . . . " he paused and I could sense his emotion growing more intense. "When my dad dies, I'm going to be pissed off at him because we didn't get our issues finished."

The group and I were stunned by the finality of the statement. It was as if Scott was already anticipating being angry at his father for the rest of his own life. Nothing was ever going to change. His father had hurt him when he was younger, and he was going to continue doing so as long as Scott lived, even after his father's death.

Now as close to tears as I'd ever seen him, Scott continued, "I didn't know he ever loved me. He'd never listen to me. Last visit when I left him at the airport, I said to myself, 'What the fuck,' and gave him a hug. You wouldn't believe it, but the old fucker hugged me back. It was the first time I could ever remember him hugging me."

OUR FAMILIES, OURSELVES

To understand ourselves as men, we must remember our relationships with our families of origin. Quite simply, it is the most powerful influence on our lives. If we fail to understand our family history, we are bound to repeat its patterns.

Many of the men I just described had come to therapy because they found themselves repeating the past, even though they were unaware of the connection. Another client, Gabe, left his wife at age forty-three to have an affair. Trouble in the marriage had surfaced when she wanted to have another child, but he refused. As part of his therapy he sought out his father, who had abandoned the family when Gabe was five. In his search Gabe learned from his father that he, too, had left at age forty-three to have an affair. The conflict in his parents' marriage had been about having another child, a fact that Gabe had never known.

Frank was a successful chemist with one major problem, voyeurism. When he finally told his older sister about the problem, she revealed that she, too, had problems with her sexuality. She revealed, to Frank's surprise, that their father had been a collector of pornography and had had numerous affairs.

Stan's wife threatened to leave him because he had become increasingly withdrawn. Then Stan learned that his real father was someone other than the man who had raised him. At the group's urging, he sought and eventually found his real father, who turned out to be an extremely withdrawn man, quite similar to Stan.

These men and others like them did not see their relationships with their families of origin as part of the cause of their problems. They tended to attribute their problems to more immediate causes, blaming either themselves ("I can't follow through on a commitment," "I can't communicate effectively," "I'm a terrible person and a sexual pervert," "I'm a complete failure who will never be able to open up emotionally with a woman again") or others ("My wife is overcontrolling," "I was sexually abused by an older man," "My wife has grown too fat"). But once they started therapy and joined the group, they began to understand the connection between family of origin and their own behavior.

CONFUSION OVER FAMILY

One of the biggest obstacles a man faces in dealing with his family of origin is his sense of confusion about whether to stay close or to move away emotionally. Many men felt uncomfortable with their families and wanted to escape as soon as they were old enough, but they still felt a strong sense of loyalty to that family. Ken, for example, was constantly making jokes about his "wacky" family. But he would become upset if someone else made a joke about or criticized his family. "It's all right if I make fun of them, but I feel the need to protect them if someone else 'messes' with them," Ken said.

This sense of loyalty runs deep. In the song "Officer Krupke," the Jets in *West Side Story* can joke with one another about all the problems in their families: drug abuse, homosexuality, poverty, physical abuse. But let one of the rival gang members cast aspersions, and they're ready to rumble.

Another source of confusion about family of origin has to do with the definition of "normal" family. Many men felt that theirs was the only "abnormal" family in the neighborhood. Consequently they would never talk to their friends about any family problems. Neither would their friends reveal family problems. This reticence thus perpetuated the myth of the "normal" family.

Sometimes I assign my clients the task of seeking out boyhood friends with whom they had lost contact over the years. Mike took the assignment to heart and found three of his high school buddies. In therapy Mike had learned the importance of starting to tell the truth about his own childhood, which included growing up with an alcoholic father. Mike returned to our session in shock. It turned out that all three of his high school buddies had also grown up in alcoholic households. Like Mike, they had kept quiet about the drinking out of a sense of shame. Each thought that he was the only one with this dark shadow to hide. This new reality gave Mike a tremendous sense of relief. At last he did not feel alone.

These revelations pinpoint another source of confusion about family of origin. Each family has an in-house reality and a community reality. What goes on behind closed doors may be very different from what the community at large sees. Bill said everyone believed his family was a pillar of the community. "My mother was the head of the PTA; my father, a farmer, was head of the Grange. People thought he planted his rows the straightest. No one suspected that when I went off to seminary at age thirteen, it was to escape from his alcoholic rages."

This internal-external discrepancy leads many boys to shut down emotionally. To the world their families are wonderful, but inside the four walls the boys are treated miserably. The pressure to be manly prevents them from talking with anyone about the home atmosphere. Many reach the erroneous conclusion that their mistreatment must be their own fault. If they weren't such a bad person, Father (or Mother) — held in such high esteem in the community — wouldn't treat them so badly.

UNGRIEVED LOSSES

The natural rhythm of living in a family includes experiencing loss. Grandparents die; pets die; eventually parents die. For some this loss occurs prematurely. The early loss of a parent can have a devastating psychological impact on children. The loss is traumatic for boys because they live under strong mandates to be "strong little soldiers," to be "big boys" and not cry, and to be a source of support to the surviving parent, especially to the mother if it is the father who has died. Men who have lost a parent early in life seem to have a particularly difficult time in their relationships with their families of origin. If the loss is not adequately grieved, its impact can be felt in the next generation. John's story illustrates this intergenerational pattern.

John's father died at age thirty-five when he drove into an embankment after midnight while returning from a late business meeting. Twenty-eight years later, when John came to my office, he was "driving" himself to an early death by working more than a hundred hours a week. A near miss as he dozed off behind the wheel late one night woke him abruptly out of his deep sleep. With a jolt he recognized that if he did not change his life-style, he, too, might not be alive at age thirty-five.

The mandate, "Big boys don't cry" leaves a trail of ungrieved losses for males. Grief is the key emotion men need to experience if they are to awaken from the deep sleep. The grief work can take many forms, including reconnecting with the memory of a lost parent; visiting the cemetery; writing a letter to a deceased parent; reconnecting with a lost parent's family (sisters, brothers, cousins); revisiting the time of the death through hypnosis or focused attention. But whatever approach we take, the grief work, while initially painful and often frightening, can be tremendously liberating. Men who find the courage to grieve describe themselves as feeling like they've come out of the shadow into the light.

FATHER HUNGER

Fathers and mothers may also simply disappear. Perhaps more common than the death of a parent is the experience of being abandoned either totally or partially by a parent. The most common forms of abandonment are divorce and birth out of wedlock. The most likely parent to leave is, of course, the father.

Here, too, a significant loss remains ungrieved. Since the father does not actually die, the child is never thought of as needing to grieve. The child usually believes the parent will return someday. Sometimes this does occur. The father might reappear briefly in the child's life, raising his hope that the father will remain there permanently. The child's hope is lifted only to be dashed as the father leaves again.

The phenomenon of the vanishing father remains widespread. In a study of one thousand children in disrupted families nationwide from 1976 to 1987, researchers found that overall 42 percent of the children had not seen their fathers at all in the previous year. "Only 20 percent slept at their father's house in a typical month, and only one in six saw the father once a week or more on the average." (Children living apart from the mother constituted a much smaller percentage, representing one of nine single-parent households, with only 7 percent not having seen their mothers in the previous year.)

The study's findings challenged some of our more conventional views of the problem of father absence. For instance, fathers who had been divorced were just as likely to stay away as fathers who had never married. There was also little difference among races: "In the study, 60 percent of the black fathers had not seen their children in the previous year compared to 47 percent of the white fathers" (from "Father's Vanishing Act Called a Common Drama," *New York Times,* June 4, 1990).

Although many divorced fathers contend that they do not see their children because their ex-wives interfere, the research does not necessarily uphold this view. Incompatibility between the parents is obviously a problem (or they wouldn't have separated), but it is not the major cause of the father's absence. "Men regard marriage as a package deal," the researcher Frank Furstenberg states. "They cannot separate their relations with their children from relations with their former spouse. When that relationship ends, the paternal bond usually withers within a few years, too."

The problem for children is not only psychological but economic. Federal statistics show that eighteen billion dollars of owed child support remains unpaid. Children raised in single-parent households with their mothers tend to be far worse off economically than those raised in homes with both parents.

This hunger for the presence of the father is not caused only by his physical absence. Fathers (and mothers) may live in the home physically but nevertheless be psychologically absent. There are three variations of this disappearance.

1. The father who is in the deep sleep.   This is the father who fits many of the characteristics described in chapter 1. He is unavailable emotionally, there but not there. Because he is not emotionally conscious himself, he has difficulty tuning in to the nuances of his child's emotional life. He is also cut off from his family of origin, perpetuating the pattern of intergenerational failure of fathering. Because the father did not have a relationship with his own father, he has no role model for interacting with his own children. Jim's father was an example of a father in the deep sleep. "My father hardly ever said a word," Jim recalled. "He'd come home, read his newspaper while the rest of the family ate, then he'd watch the news on TV. He had no friends, no interests other than work. He'd never ask me anything about myself." (Many of these men may also be classified as depressed.)

2. The workaholic father.   This type of father is rarely around. In the old days this father's excessive patterns of work were viewed as necessary for the survival of the family. In the 1950s this pattern was viewed as normal, particularly given the uncertainty of the economy. The philosophy was: If there's work available, take as much of it as possible. He works a regular shift, then overtime, then maybe a second job. Often he has no choice—overtime is mandatory in blue-collar jobs; white-collar jobs require excessive hours to ensure promotion. But whether the excessive work patterns are forced or voluntary, the effect on the children is much the same. They miss their father. Either he isn't there at all or he comes home in a foul mood because of the stresses of the workplace. This pattern is devastating for sons because their role model, their same-sex parent, is unavailable. Boys are left to be raised by mothers, by women, whom boys are trying not to be like.

3. *The alcoholic or violent father.*   The third type of father who creates feelings of longing on the part of his children is the alcoholic father. Like the father in the deep sleep, he is there but not there. Whenever he is there his children wonder whether he is under the influence of alcohol. The man they know as father is often alien, a man in an altered state. Growing up with an alcoholic father is like growing up with a Dr. Jekyll and Mr. Hyde character. From day to day his children don't know which father to expect. If he is an early stage of daily drinking, he can be cheerful and accessible; if we catch him after he has had one too many, he can be frightening, capable of inflicting psychological or physical wounds.

Scott had an alcoholic father. When he had too much to drink, he'd line up all the boys in the family and rap them on their heads with his knuckles. If one boy did something wrong, all the kids were punished. When his father was due home, Scott would retreat to his bedroom and keep score of the Tiger game. If his father came home drunk, Scott hoped he would forget that Scott was back there. If Scott was playing outside, he'd have to pass his father to get back in, which meant risking his father's physical aggression.

Not all alcoholic fathers are physically cruel. Some erupt only with criticism. Mike remembers that he could never please his alcoholic father. No matter how hard he'd try, it was never good enough. Any failure would be greeted with scorn and derision. Often the criticism would be sarcastic in nature, "I always knew you weren't as bright as your brother, but now I'm not sure you're as smart as your cat." Since Mike's father rarely became obviously drunk, he never associated the criticism with drinking. When he first began therapy, Mike denied that his father was alcoholic. Only when he realized that he almost never saw his father when he was not under the influence of alcohol did Mike begin to think differently. "He always had a few beers as soon as he got home from work at 6:30," Mike recounted. "On Saturdays he'd work until six and then would drink more heavily when he and my mother went out with friends. Sunday morning he didn't drink, but I guess he was hung over from Saturday night. Then when football came on Sunday afternoon he'd begin again. And so it would go, week in, week out for as long as I can remember. Now that he's older, it's more obvious what the effects of the alcohol are. His personality changes as soon as he has a drink."

Part of Mike's reluctance to classify his father as an alcoholic is that Mike's wife began to question his own drinking patterns. Mike denies that he is an alcoholic, but his drinking patterns are remarkably similar to his father's, only Mike restricts his drinking to five days a week instead of seven. When we did a family of origin comparison, Mike was clearly upset by having to confront the similarities.

Mike's experience is similar to those of other children of alcoholics. They themselves sometimes become alcoholics. This is one of the most pervasive and disturbing patterns we see in therapy. Having known the horrors of growing up in an alcoholic household, they find it hard to imagine how they could have become alcoholics themselves. Mike developed an alcohol problem as an adult, as did two of his brothers. This was after vowing that he would never drink. He also developed other addictions, to marijuana, work, and sex. How can we understand this phenomenon?

Some would argue that alcohol is a genetically linked disease. Certainly the research indicates the presence of some genetic component in the disease of alcoholism — people with a certain genetic makeup react differently to alcohol than others do. But this is not true for everyone. Clearly some psychological factors also affect the situation.

Most alcoholic families rely on denial of the problem as a survival mechanism. This process of denial has been written about extensively in the literature on alcoholism and adult children of alcoholics. Because the family relies on denial, the child's reality is denied as well. Scott may have experienced abuse, but he believed that it was not abuse but "correction" for his terrible behavior. His parents were just trying to straighten him out for his own good, much as they were trying to train their puppy by swatting it with a rolled-up newspaper.

Along with his reality, Scott's feelings were also denied. If he said he felt lonely, he was told that he shouldn't feel lonely because he had brothers to play with.

If he said he was hungry, he was told he just ate and should be thankful that he wasn't living in India. If he was scared and looked like he might cry, he was told to stop or he would really be given something to cry about.

As he grew older Scott learned to deny his own reality. When he had a feeling, he learned to question its validity. "Should I feel this way or not?" he'd ask himself, as if a feeling had a rational mind. Later he learned to suppress his feelings altogether. Usually he was successful, but occasionally he became wound tight as a knot in his efforts to suppress his feelings. When the tension became unbearable, he'd look for relief.

He had learned that a man turns to alcohol, sex, and marijuana for relief — these were outlets available to a young man in the 1960s. Knowing his father abused alcohol, he convinced himself he could be smarter, stronger, wiser. He would use it only when he needed it. At first he was successful at controlling it. But as pressures to perform at college and eventually in corporate life grew, so did his problems.

I believe that Scott never had the opportunity to grieve his father's alcoholism and the pain he consequently suffered. If he had gained awareness of the problem and had grieved, he might have been able to avoid repeating the destructive patterns. His early sense of reality might have been confirmed. His feelings might have been validated. He might have acknowledged the truth and been able to stop living a lie.

Unfortunately it was not until many years later, years during which he followed his father's reality and hated himself for doing so, that Scott had the truth confirmed and was ready to face the challenges of change.

CONFUSION OVER MOTHER

After devoting several group sessions to fathers, I decided to switch the topic to mothers. The men seemed almost relieved, eager to talk about their mothers. The tension and anger that had so dominated the group when we talked about fathers seemed to diminish. Whereas fathers had to be pursued, mothers were (almost) always there.

It was as if the men were always longing to join their fathers as they disappeared daily to work but were uncertain whether they wanted to leave the security of the mother. It felt safe, secure, warm. There their needs were met. Yet they were uncertain whether they felt protected or trapped. To pursue the father meant taking risks; it was frightening. To stay with mother was safe; but was it manly? How could they feel independent and autonomous in the safety of Mother's care?

I began the group by asking the men to think of metaphors describing their mothers. Arnie started. "My mother is my number one fan," he said. "She's my personal cheerleader. She's behind me no matter what I do."

Rick was ambivalent about his mother. "She's the mystery woman. She'd never get up to fix us breakfast or send us off to school like the other mothers did. She'd be a different person each day when we came home from school. I never knew what to expect. When my mother came into the room, I'd look closely at her. When she raised her hand, I didn't know whether she was going to hug me or hit me."

Phil's mother died when he was a teenager. "I knew my mother hadn't been Donna Reed, but that's what I wanted: a pretty woman in a shirtwaist dress who had a smile for a greeting and supper on the table every night."

Tom said he really had a mother like that. "My mom was there. She faithfully played the role of mother, but she wasn't happy or warm. She turns out to be a much warmer grandmother to my niece than I ever remember her being as a mother."

Scott was the most protective of his mother. "My dad would hit my mother. As each of us boys grew up, we took turns trying to protect her from Dad's violence. We always wished she would leave him, and one time she even did. She piled us all in the car in the middle of the day and drove us to a motel. We stayed for a few days, but then the money ran out, and dad kept calling saying how sorry he was and how he'd never hit her again. Before I knew it we were back home and the whole thing started over again."

When Mike asked him how it was now with his mother and father, Scott went on, "They're finally divorced now, but I still feel like I've got to protect my mother. I never tell her about my problems because I don't think she'll be able to handle it. She's too brittle. It's like she'll fall apart if she knows I've got problems."

This rang true also for Derrick. "I was raised by my mother. After my father left we moved up north, and she raised all of us on her own. Every morning she'd get up before us and start dinner. Then she'd take three buses to work. She'd be back at five to finish the dinner she'd started in the morning. As the eldest, I became a substitute for my father. I was always her 'little man.' I felt responsible, so I went out and started earning money by sweeping floors when I was eleven. Mom always told me she loved me, but now I can see she was manipulative. She wanted me to behave in certain ways. She still tried to control my life in many ways. When I go home now I'm careful not to share too much with her or she'll try to tell me what to do."

The men were surprised by the depth of their feelings during this initial go-round in the group. The session had turned quite serious. Perhaps they felt as much confusion about mothers as they did about fathers. Certainly, they noted, it wasn't all baseball, mom, and apple pie. The images portrayed on TV of the all-devoted, affectionate, loving, understanding mother did not fit their realities. As we moved deeper into the discussion, it became clear to these men that their mothers tended not to be entirely happy or comfortable with their roles.

These men were describing the mothers of the baby-boom generation. They were the mothers who after World War II moved to pretty little homes in the suburbs, where they were supposed to raise a slew of kids while their husbands went off to work. But as the group reflected on the topic, they began to understand why twenty years later some women of that generation were becoming interested in the women's liberation movement and why others had suffered from depression during their lives.

My own mother was a typical example of women of that generation. As a young woman in the Great Depression, she was forced to work rather than study acting and singing, her true loves. As World War II started she married my father a few days before he went off for four years to serve in the Persian Gulf. Surprisingly, as she talks to me now about her personal history, these were four of the best years of her life. On her own for the first time in her life, she traveled all over the United States by train. Once again she was able to perform as a singer on local radio shows. She made enough money to survive and even to save a little. All the while she was receiving letters from my father, who described his postwar dream: to buy her a little house and to make enough money to make her happy, and, of course, to have children (he even named me Robbie in the letters). She wasn't sure about his dream. Besides missing him and being worried about the war, she was feeling good being an independent woman making her own contribution to the war cause.

But when my dad returned home, it was his dream they pursued. Just like her sister and all her cousins, my mother had a child (me) within a year. Within five years she was living in a suburban house — a half mile down a dirt road to the nearest bus — with no car and few neighbors. She had always been an urban woman, loving the bustle of the big city, but now she was part of the New American Dream, and she was supposed to be happy, safely ensconced in the suburbs.

Yet she didn't feel safe and happy. Instead she felt unfulfilled and lonely. All the outlets she had enjoyed during the war were now closed off to her: the good jobs were reserved for the returning male soldiers, she was expected to raise children, not to travel and be a performer. It was like a new version of being kept barefoot and pregnant; now it was married with children in the suburbs.

Approaching their adolescence, boys of the baby-boom generation, raised primarily by their mothers, craved distance from Mother. Autonomy and independence was their dream. Yet for many women mothering was their primary role. They were not eager to give up their sons (and daughters). The boys sought distance, the mothers wanted to continue to protect. They were engaged in the classic mother-son struggle, a push-pull struggle for dependence and autonomy that many men know so well. Many men not only played it out with their mothers but continued it with the women they married. Fortunately my mother and I were able to achieve a satisfactory resolution of the mother-son struggle during a ten-year period that started when I went away to college.

In my senior year of college I met my wife, an independent and extremely competent woman. For over twenty years we have worked together to try to create new patterns in our family that are based on ideals of equality and cooperation. The road of change has not always been easy. Despite our best efforts, my spouse, who has a successful career in her own right, still does more of the child care and housework than I do.

Generally it is so common for the paradigms established in the family of origin to repeat themselves in the next generation that we are almost blind to the process. Recognizing the connection between past patterns and current patterns is like opening your eyes as you begin to awaken from the deep sleep.

4 LEARNING TO RECOGNIZE AND TRUST OUR FEELINGS

"When I first came for therapy I thought there were two emotions," said one of my clients. "You could feel good or you could feel bad."

As men we have been raised to distrust our feelings. At an early age we were taught that to show emotional vulnerability was a sign of weakness. Because life is a series of ups and downs, however, to hide our natural responses carries considerable risk.

Take the case of Sean, who came to see me during his freshman year of college. When he was fifteen years old and a sophomore in high school, his mother, a well-known business owner in town, abruptly left the family. One day she was there, the next day she had packed her clothes and left the house. Sean was devastated. His emotions were a wild mass of confusion: anger over the abandonment; fear about how his father was going to cope with the loss; shame over his mother leaving so suddenly; and of course grief over the loss of his mother, whom he would see only once a week.

Despite the intense pain, Sean believed he was not supposed to show that he was hurting. He believed that to be a strong man meant going on with his life as if nothing happened. He continued to play baseball, to go to school, to date his girlfriend. When his teachers or coaches asked how he was doing, he would smile and answer, "Fine, I'm doing fine." His male friends, operating under the same set of beliefs as Sean, tended not to ask him about his feelings at all. If they detected his emotional pain, they'd leave him alone so as not to embarrass him. They believed that if Sean cried in front of them, he would only feel worse about the situation. Besides, they would not have known what to do about his tears. Instead they comforted him by keeping him busy and colluding with him on the pretense that everything was OK and he was doing just fine.

Sean believed, as his friends did, that to react emotionally to such a devastating event would only compound his losses. Not only would he have lost his mother, but his developing sense of pride in himself as a male would be shattered, too. To admit his vulnerability, to publicly acknowledge feelings or give voice to his deep emotions, would be as cowardly as bailing out on a fastball.

So as Sean went on pretending everything was OK, others watched helplessly as his grades fell, his participation in baseball tapered off, and he grew increasingly isolated. Finally, after months of insistence on his father's and mother's part, he agreed to see a psychologist, but even then with the stipulation that it be kept a secret from his friends. Even with the psychologist Sean had difficulty expressing his emotions. He remained ashamed of not being able to "just keep forging ahead" with his life. He asked the psychologist to teach him self-hypnosis "so I can learn to concentrate again and to get these stupid feelings out of my head."

Sean's wish to get those stupid feelings out of his head is typical of how we men have been raised to regard feelings.

Rather than viewing feelings as a natural, biologically based reaction to events in our lives, we have been taught to view them as a nuisance, an inconvenience, an unwelcome interloper in our lives. It is not that we are taught that feelings do not exist but rather that being a man requires us to keep our feelings under control. It is as if we harbor an internal competition between the good guys — the mind, self-discipline, rationality — and the bad guys — feelings, impulses, emotionality. The outcome of this battle determines our status as men. The judges include our parents and our peers but most of all ourselves.

This unhealthy internal struggle can confound us throughout our lives. As young men, like Sean, we struggle to learn the rules of the game. But when we later move into committed relationships, we begin to hear conflicting messages, especially from our wives, who urge us to be more expressive of our feelings. "Why can't you be more in touch with your feelings?" "Why don't you ever tell me how you feel?" "Strong men aren't afraid of their feelings."

In the workplace, however, the same old messages are reinforced. Don't let your feelings get in the way of being an effective leader. Don't be overly emotional with your clients. Just do your job and don't ask questions. What we're after is results, not your feelings.

And what do we want for ourselves? We're not often sure. After years of trying to keep our feelings at bay, by midlife we may be left clueless about our true wants and needs. We rarely trust the emotional cues available to us. Instead we follow the blueprint that society provides to determine what we need and want — a good job, possessions, prestige, and power, all earned through hard work and preferably without complaints.

Within the men's movement we are implored by such leaders as Robert Bly and Sam Keen to "go into our gut" and "to work to get the feelings out." Yet fear, an important emotion itself, causes many to pause at the precipice of the plunge into the icy waters of emotion. Men are being encouraged to venture into unknown territory, an area that has been designated as dark, dangerous, and unsafe.

The way to make this journey inward was a frequent topic of conversation for men in my male support groups.

When I first started, my therapist would say, "Well, how do you feel about such and such?" and I used to think I had two feelings, good and bad. I couldn't break down any finer feelings than that. "How do you feel?" Pretty good, or I feel bad today. Nervous was a big feeling to me. It was one of my hard ones. If I didn't feel good, I was nervous. That was it. That was my range.

It wasn't that I wasn't feeling anything, but in my marriage when I was asked how I felt, it was like I couldn't tell you how I really felt. I had to stuff what I was really feeling and pay the bills, fix whatever needed to be fixed, be the person who solved the problem, whether it was for the kids, for the wife, or whatever. The same thing was true at work.

The way I was raised we really learned to stuff our feelings down inside. I think what happens is you get to a point where you have so many feelings stuffed inside that you can't get in touch with them anymore. They are all mixed up together. Once you start to express feelings, though, it becomes easier and easier. You start to untangle these things, and as you do, there's this whole rich world that you get to experience. I know, I've spent the last twenty years of my life sleeping under a tree where I just didn't feel anything.

HOW WE KEEP OUR EMOTIONS UNDER CONTROL

Most men pay a high psychological price for the effort expended to keep their emotions under control. To estimate the cost let us first examine the ways men try to master their emotions.

At first the process entails not letting the emotions show. As boys we learned to not let others know how we feel. Although most boys are aware that they are having feelings, they generally have not developed a vocabulary for identifying what those feelings are. To let it out would be seen as a sign of weakness, especially if it was one of the negative emotions, such as fear, sadness, or shame.

To hide our feelings we learn several strategies.

- We learn to control our facial muscles ("Keep a poker face"), our voices and gait ("Walk like a man, talk like a man"); our tear ducts ("Big boys don't cry"), and our hands ("Nerves of steel").

- When we are unable to hide our feelings, we hide ourselves. As boys we learned to retreat from others when we were emotional, to go to a place where we would not be seen — usually to our rooms or to some private hiding place. As adults the pattern continues. I've been told by many male clients that they will avoid an event entirely if they believe the event will somehow provoke their emotions. Some have skipped high school reunions, weddings, or funerals because they feared they would be overcome by emotion in public.

- As we become adept at hiding our emotions, we learn to deny that our feelings affect us at all. At first we may be trying to fool others. At this stage we sense when we are reacting emotionally, but we try to perfect the act of not letting the feelings show. With practice we begin to fool ourselves. We begin to believe that we have total control over our emotions. Events happen, but we are cool, meaning that the events do not bother us at all. We strive to be like the cowboys in the old western movies, men like Gary Cooper or John Wayne, who could just do what had to be done and not let their emotions get in the way. Such men appeared to have nerves of steel, showing neither fear in the face of danger nor grief at the loss of their loved ones.

- To perfect the denial of feelings we learn increasingly sophisticated techniques. One of these is the defense of the counterattack. If somehow we are threatened or ridiculed by others, we learned to put them down or threaten them. This is "the-best-defense-is-a-good-offense" strategy. Among young boys this pattern of interaction is readily apparent. Boys boast to one another, threaten and dare one another, and put each other down unmercifully. Usually the behavior remains in the verbal realm, and often it contains elements of humor. The teasing, put-downs, and threats are rewarded with laughter.

In the movie *Goodfellas,* for instance, one hood, Tommy, tells a fellow hood, Henry, a very funny story about how tough he is. When Tommy has Henry laughing in stitches, his mood suddenly turns ugly. "What do you find so funny?" Tommy asks. "Are you laughing at me?" he wants to know. Henry is confused. Is Tommy angry at him? Did Henry suddenly go too far? Henry thought he was laughing with Tommy, not at him. Everyone is looking at Henry. Does he appear afraid? Should he apologize or defend himself? Henry decides to apologize, and when he does, Tommy turns the mood around one more time. "I got you," says Tommy. Everyone laughs, relieved. Everyone except Henry. He has been played for the fool. His task now is to not let his true feelings show. If he reveals his anger or shame, he knows he'll be viewed as a man who can't take a little ribbing, a sign of weakness.

To keep our emotions under control, men learn to ask themselves whether it is appropriate to feel a certain way, thus using the rational mind to question the emotional sides. "Do I have a right to feel this way?" or "Should I feel this way" or "Isn't it stupid to feel this way?" We learn, in essence, to talk ourselves out of our feelings.

This type of self-talk is learned at an early age and is often taught to us by our parents. Mike recalls as a child telling his parents that he was jealous of his sister on her birthday. They responded by telling him that he shouldn't feel jealous, that it was his sister's special day and he shouldn't ruin it by acting jealous. In itself this was not bad advice, but his parents went on to scold him, to tell him that he had no right to be jealous, and to threaten to spank him and banish him to his room if he didn't stop. Mike learned from this that it was not OK to have certain feelings. If he had such feelings, he should get them under control, talk himself out of them, or else suffer the consequences.

What is wrong with this type of reasoning? Feelings themselves are not the problem. It is the behavior associated with the feelings that can lead to trouble. Mike did not learn that jealousy was a normal, expected response to a sibling's birthday. Instead he was made to feel ashamed for feeling jealous. It would not have been appropriate for Mike to act out jealous feelings by ruining his sister's presents. But in this case he merely told his parents how he felt. For this he was made to feel ashamed.

This confusion about the distinction between feelings and action is typical for men. As boys we learned that the feelings themselves were bad. What we now know is that a feeling is just that — a feeling. What we do have control over is how we react to our feelings. If we feel jealous, so be it. But if we destroy things out of our jealousy, we are acting in an inappropriate manner.

The self-talk men conduct about their feelings often fails to take into account this important distinction. Instead of acknowledging our feelings as valuable parts of ourselves, instead of trusting our feelings as important parts of our decision-making process, instead of honoring our feelings as much as we honor our rational thinking, we have learned to dismiss, distrust, and be disgusted with our feelings.

THE CONSEQUENCES OF NOT TRUSTING OUR FEELINGS

What are the consequences of not trusting our feelings? How does the overemphasis on our rational sides and this distrust of our emotional sides lead to trouble for us as men? There are several consequences.

1. Not knowing how we feel leads to confusion about what we truly need in our lives. If we are not sure how we feel about things in our lives — about people, our jobs, our community — we'll have difficulty envisioning what we need to make us happy. If we don't know how we feel in the present, how can we project how we will feel in the future? If we don't know how we will feel, how can we be clear about what we want to establish as goals for the future?

For many men this confusion results in following a path that is dictated to us by the norms of our society rather than by our own inner feelings. Many midlife crises stem from our decisions to pursue wealth and prestige rather than our interests, that is, those endeavors that truly make us *feel* fulfilled.

2. *Bottled-up emotions throw off the healthy balance of our lives.* As youngsters we learned that a show of emotion was a sign of defeat or weakness. There are only a few exceptions to the mandate to keep emotions under control. One is the show of anger, which we will discuss later in this chapter. The other is the show of emotion over a victory. When the Chicago Bulls won their first NBA championship, Michael Jordan cried on national television after the victory. The nation viewed these tears as acceptable, even appropriate. Yet a year later when Chris Webber, a freshman at the University of Michigan, cried after his team lost in the NCAA finals, he wrapped his head in a towel to hide his tears.

Likewise after the cease-fire in the Persian Gulf War, General Norman Schwartzkopf could show grief for the U.S. soldiers who had been killed. But to grieve so during the battle would have been unacceptable, because it may have given the enemy the idea that he was soft, sensitive, not stern enough in his emotional resolve.

In many work settings a high value is placed on being in emotional control. To say what you feel may endanger one's position. Men who are trying to become more emotionally open may be viewed with suspicion or even with derision. One male client who enjoyed the more open

emotionality of a men's group tried to strike up an emotionally honest conversation with a colleague at work.
Each time he shared something personal, the colleague
accused him of trying to play psychiatrist. Other men
report similar reactions. Open emotionality in the workplace remains largely unacceptable.

Unfortunately the highly competitive nature of most
work settings may require one to stay closed emotionally.
To be open may make the worker vulnerable. A "competitor" may use his open colleague's honest revelations
against him.

Neal revealed to a colleague that he was feeling
burned-out at work and wished he could spend more time
at home with his children. A few weeks later, on a beautiful summer day, Neal went to work late and left a little
early. He also went for a walk during his lunch break. As
Neal was leaving work that day, his colleague eyed him
and commented facetiously, "Aren't you a man of leisure
— strolling in late, taking a siesta, then leaving whenever
you want." Neal was angry, but he kept it to himself, at
least until he got home and could talk it over with his wife.

3. *Through ignoring our feelings we grow out of touch with
our bodies.* Emotions express themselves through our
bodies. We literally feel or experience emotions in various
places in our bodies. We feel emotions as a wave in our gut
or a lump in the throat or shaky hands or a pain in our
heart or a tear in our eye.

When we learn to suppress our emotions, we are
learning to ignore these bodily sensations. Through this
process of ignoring our bodily sensations, we gradually
begin to lose touch with our bodies.

One major consequence of losing touch with our bodies is that we neglect our health. Pain is one way the body communicates to the brain that something is wrong somewhere. As men we know we are supposed to play through or ignore the pain. Yet ignoring pain can put us at risk.

Doctors report that men often wait much longer than women to seek medical attention for pain or discomfort. Even when they do go to the doctor, they tend to minimize their symptoms. They may report symptoms of a heart attack, for example, as "minor discomfort." As a consequence, men often are sicker than women before visiting the doctor and require more drastic medical intervention. This pattern of ignoring pain, which is related to ignoring feelings, may be an important factor in men's shorter life spans.

In the 1991 All-Star baseball game I observed two examples of how men are held up as heroes for playing through pain. That year was the fiftieth anniversary of a famous catch by Ted Williams, a baseball legend. In the 1941 All-Star game he crashed into a wall while making a spectacular catch. Fifty years later Williams was still being described in superlative terms for having played the game with a broken arm.

In the 1991 game the pitcher Jack Morris was hit on the foot by a line drive. He went down in a lump but came up smiling, apparently unfazed by the blow. He finished out the inning and pitched the next inning as well. A few innings later he was interviewed, wearing street clothes, on the way to the hospital for X-rays. The interviewer asked how he had pitched with such a serious injury and why he had jumped up smiling. "I smiled so Tony [his manager] wouldn't know I was hurt. If he did, he'd take me out of the game." The announcer laughed at how clever (and brave) Jack had been to fool his manager.

Is it any wonder that the thousands of school boys watching the game would learn that ignoring bodily sensations and playing through the pain is the right way to act as a man?

4. We do not learn a language for expressing feelings.   As males the language we learn is the language of competition and achievement. As the linguist Deborah Tannen so aptly illustrates in her book *You Just Don't Understand* (New York: William Morrow, 1990), men and women learn essentially two different languages to express themselves. Women tend to communicate in the language of emotion, while men use the language of competition. This language works very well in the work setting, but it places us at a distinct disadvantage in relationships. Many men simply do not have a vocabulary to describe their feelings. If asked how they feel, they tend to give a response that reflects how they think about a situation.

Phil's wife was afraid of losing her job. I asked him how he would feel if she was to lose her job, which accounted for one half of the couple's income.

PHIL: I'd feel that she'd have no trouble finding another.

ME: That's what you predict would happen. I'm asking how you would feel about it.

PHIL: I know. I'd feel that we'd do just fine.

ME: What would be your emotional reaction to her losing her job?

PHIL: I'm telling you I don't feel it would happen, and if it did, we'd cope.

Phil could have more appropriately substituted the word think for the word *feel*. He simply did not have available a list of words that would describe his feelings.

When a man says, "I only know of two feelings, good and bad," he's not kidding. When we work on feelings in group sessions, men have asked me to put a list of the most common feelings on the board.

One night a man brought a variety of gourmet cheeses to the group. There was smoked Gouda, Emmentaler, and Brie, among others. The topic of discussion was feelings. One man commented that his knowledge of feelings was like his knowledge of cheese. For a long time he thought there were two types of cheese — Swiss and Velveeta. Now that he's learning about other varieties of cheese, a whole new world is opening up to him. Likewise as he learns new words and meanings for feelings, he's opening to parts of himself he never experienced before.

Another illustration from the group shows how men learn through the group process to begin to develop their emotional vocabulary.

We were well into the evening's group, past the time when we were reporting on "how we felt and what we needed" when Tom said he wanted to ask Phil a question. "I know you lost your mother when you were young and your father just recently. Last week my mother was in the hospital. My question is, Do you worry about your mortality?"

Phil seemed surprised and didn't know how to answer the question. Then Arnie intervened. "Tom," he said, "you're telling us that your mother might be on her deathbed. You hadn't even mentioned this tonight, yet now you're asking Phil if he thinks about his mortality. Where are your own feelings about what happened to your mother? What about her mortality . . . or yours?"

After several minutes of intense conversation, Tom and the group began to realize what had occurred. Tom had experienced a severe trauma. His mother had almost died. He had reacted with a confusing mixture of feelings: fear, helplessness, guilt, and anger, among others. Yet until he began talking in the group, he was unaware of these feelings, almost numb to them. Furthermore, at a time of need he could think of no one to call to support him. Playing the role of the strong son helping his mother, Tom did not consider how emotionally draining it had been to sit by his mother's side in intensive care. When he came to the group, he knew he wanted to talk about what had happened, but he did not know how to begin. He feared being open about his feelings, and he didn't know why. Perhaps he thought he had no right to feel the way he did. After all, it was his mother's illness, not his. Perhaps he feared that the others wouldn't support him, or, worse yet, they'd feel too sorry for him.

Whatever the reason, Tom chose a very indirect way to tell us about his trauma, so indirect that if one of the group members had not picked up on it, we may have missed it entirely.

This incident demonstrates how difficult it is for men to express their feelings at a time of need. Somehow we have come to learn that at a time of crisis we are the ones who are supposed to be strong. Our feelings and needs are not important. What is important is our strength and ability to not let our emotions get in the way. For Tom this meant not acknowledging how scared he was of losing his mother or how guilty he felt about not being near her when she became ill (he had been away on business) or how lonely he felt sitting in intensive care for two days, helplessly watching his mother.

The more Tom talked, the more trusting of the group he felt. The group members wished he had called them for support. Rather than feeling put out, they would have felt honored that he had thought of them. At the end of the conversation, Phil asked him if he felt like crying at any time during the trauma. Tom replied, "I don't know how to cry, but I did feel a knot in my stomach during the whole weekend. Maybe I wish I could have cried. Maybe it would have helped."

5. *When we do not acknowledge our hurts or losses, we do not grieve and so end up carrying our pain with us for a long time.*   If we can't express our feelings, we can't purge ourselves of painful memories. Talking about humiliations helps to purify them of their toxicity. If we keep them to ourselves, holding them as our private secrets, we multiply our shame about them. But if we reveal these past hurts to ourselves and someone else, we defuse their power.

One of the main functions of men's groups is to enable participants to talk about their past hurts. Many men have never told anyone about such incidents or listened to another man tell about his own. It's as if we've grown up in a male cult of secrecy. If we can't rid ourselves of the hurt, we assume our own character weakness or effeminacy is to blame. Therefore we hide it. Because most men are hiding their feelings of humiliation, each man believes he is alone in trying to hide those feelings. No one wants to be the first to break this code of secrecy.

In the men's groups the code is finally broken. What a tremendous relief it is for men to be able to share with one another the pain of past hurts and to realize that they are not the only ones who have had such experiences.

Inevitably the men will begin talking to each other about the physical punishments they received as children.

Most men now approaching middle age were reared with the "Spare the rod, spoil the child" dictum. Even though physical punishments were common, they had a traumatic effect on the men. As men begin to talk about the physical punishments they received from their parents, they do so at first in almost humorous tones: "Boy, do I remember getting it from my father when I came home late one night from a football game." But as they begin to reveal more detail about the event, their pain and humiliation begin to pour out. "You wouldn't believe it. He hit me with a fucking baseball bat. He forced me to bend over and hit me with this wooden bat across my legs. I wanted to kill the S.O.B., but I knew I couldn't let him know it hurt me. That was my revenge."

Not being able to react emotionally to the physical punishment caused psychic scarring that lasts much longer than the bruises. As the men talk about the physical traumas, it is as if they were back in the scene still experiencing themselves as young, helpless boys. The humiliation of being hit and yet having to "take it like a man" was a doubly traumatic blow.

One of the most troubling effects of physical punishment is that its victims tend in turn to become physically hurtful to others. Many men's group members recall beating up other boys and getting into gang fights. They may be physically violent with women and may use physical punishment with their own children. Most child and spouse abusers were physically abused as children, and most men who are sexual abusers were sexually abused as children.

Talking about this dark side of the male psyche, although extremely difficult, can be tremendously beneficial. For far too long there has been a conspiracy of silence about the abuse of men and its repercussions. It is a painful and highly controversial topic. Men who have been abusive resent being lumped in as statistics when violent crime, rape, and spouse and child abuse rates are reported. Yet we must find ways to begin to discuss openly the appalling impact of abuse on our society.

6. *As a consequence of trying to control our feelings, we become less sensitive to the feelings of others.* Empathy means being sensitive to the feelings of others, the ability to put ourselves in someone else's shoes and to experience feelings as the other person does. Yet if we grow up with the notion that we are supposed to be effective at competing with others, we find it difficult to concern ourselves with how our competitor feels. In many ways we don't want to know how he or she feels, because it would make us feel uncomfortable to know that this person is hurting. If we become too concerned about "not hurting someone's feelings," we might not be aggressive enough in trying to defeat that person.

Empathy is generally not a high priority in male socialization, especially compared with female development. For males the primary objective is to compete. For females it is to develop and maintain relationships. Empathy is valuable in the development of relationships, but it is an impediment to competition. It is not helpful to have to worry over what your opponent will feel about being defeated.

Of course not all males lack empathy. There are in fact many empathetic men in the world. The problem is, though, that many of these empathetic men do not see their empathy as a virtue. Some even consider it a drawback. A graduating law student came to see me for help recently. He was worried that he was too sensitive about the feelings of others. He wanted to know if I could help him "toughen up mentally." When I asked for clarification, he explained that he feared he would be too sensitive, too nice, on his first job as a lawyer. He had a sense that management wanted him to be "leaner and meaner." He feared he would not be able to make tough decisions because he was "too hung up on not offending anyone." In essence he was asking me to tone down his empathetic side and bolster his aggressive side.

When I balked at his request and pointed out how his empathy could be a virtue, he balked at therapy. At age twenty-four he believed he needed a tougher skin to survive. Perhaps he was right. In his field, like many occupations men choose, emotional toughness, not sensitivity, is a requirement.

7. *We develop strategies for managing our emotions that are detrimental to our families or significant relationships.* We are raised to be managers of our emotions rather than expressors of our emotions. Many of these management strategies are adaptive in the workplace but disastrous in intimate relationships.

Foremost among these maladaptive strategies is learning to delay our emotional reactions. Often we experience feelings, especially anger, that we cannot express at work. Most of us work in a hierarchical setting and we learn that we are supposed to take orders from those ranked higher in the organizational chart. We are not supposed to protest or react emotionally to orders received. So we learn to take the orders without showing emotion, this does not mean that we do not have feelings about being ordered around. We learn to delay our feelings — delay our reactions — until we are dealing with someone lower or equal in rank. We dump our emotional frustration on these people.

We may also delay this emotional reaction until we return home, then express it toward a spouse or child. If a man is aware of his frustrations from work, he may be able to talk them over civilly with his wife and release his feelings peacefully. But if he is not aware of his frustrations, they may come out sideways — through irritability or anger at home. Robert Bly talks about this as "men bringing home their mood." After a day of having to delay emotional reactions, of having to sit on their feelings while at work, men find it far too convenient to let these feelings out in the comfort and safety of home.

Another emotional-management strategy that can be detrimental is withdrawing rather than reacting emotionally. This strategy also has two sides. On the one hand we learn that it is better to go off by ourselves to try to calm down rather than to blow up at someone. On the other hand we find that the easiest way to avoid a blowup is to minimize engagement with other people. This strategy of withdrawal quickly becomes a maladaptive pattern. What began as a useful emotional-management strategy ends up as estrangement and isolation.

Harry, for example, tended to snipe at his wife and children after a day at the plant. He didn't like this irritable part of himself and recognized that he was taking out his frustrations from work on his family at home. Yet he didn't know what to do with the emotional buildup. He didn't know how to relax. Each day he would read the paper, check the mail, and watch the news on TV. Usually he would have a beer or two. As long as no one demanded his attention, he managed not to grouch or complain. But when his wife or children tried to talk to him about anything difficult, he showed little patience. If they persisted, he was quick to yell at them or to say something critical.

To control these outbursts he taught himself to walk away from others before he became too angry, lost his temper, and said something he later regretted. He would go to his bedroom, workshop, or just take a walk. By getting away he was able to manage his emotions.

The only trouble with this strategy was that other family members experienced it as rejection. They began describing Harry's retreat as his "disappearing act." They complained that he was never available, that he was touchy, that they could never find the right time to discuss things with him.

They were at an impasse. Harry had adopted withdrawal as a mechanism for managing his emotions. It worked as a means to keep his emotions under control. But for the rest of the family, his solution had become the problem. They missed Harry as a husband and father and viewed his withdrawal as a personal rejection.

8. *We rely on potentially addictive substances to help us manage our emotions.* For many men addictive substances, especially alcohol and marijuana, serve important functions in the management of emotions. Perhaps most significantly they offer a way to relax. Both alcohol and marijuana have the effect of relieving anxiety, one of the most uncomfortable emotions men experience.

The use of both of these is highly ritualized. Regular users of alcohol tend to have a routine of where and when they drink. For many it is a drink after work, either at a bar or at home. Others ritualize alcohol consumption around meals — a beer or a glass of wine or two with dinner. Whatever the ritual, alcohol use becomes so automatic that one is not aware of making a choice about its consumption. It becomes a habit, a routine way for stopping the work day and beginning "relaxation," a way to close down unpleasant emotions.

RECOGNIZING TWO KEY EMOTIONS: GRIEF AND ANGER

Trying to sort out our feelings can be confusing, because often we experience not just one emotion but a combination of several. In my years of work with men I have found it useful to begin work on emotional sensitivity by focusing on two key emotions that seem to be the most problematic ones for men: grief and anger.

Grief

This emotion deals with loss. It is what we feel when we lose someone, something, or even a goal. Grief is the process we go through in the aftermath of that loss. Our problem is that our grief is often short-circuited. We have not been allowed, or do not allow ourselves, adequate time to grieve over our losses. Beginning with boyhood and continuing throughout the life cycle, we are told that the appropriate way to handle loss of any kind is to acknowledge it stoically then to get on with life, quickly, which usually means acting like the loss never occurred.

This simply does not work. If a loss is not adequately mourned, it can have adverse effects on a person's psychological development, particularly on the way the person behaves in future relationships.

I see a number of men in my practice who as boys lost a parent. When the parent died, the boy believed he was supposed to be strong and to conceal his emotions. If it was the father who died, the boy experienced another bur-

den and obstacle to his grief: He believed he was supposed
to take his father's place, to act like a "little man," to be
like a replacement husband for his mother. "Son, you
have to be a man now. Your mother needs you now that
your father's gone." Although people do not usually mean
this literally, a boy may take it quite seriously.

Peter's father died when he was nine. As the eldest of
three young children, the role of father replacement fell to
him. He remembers only a few of the details from this
period, but he does recall that his father was seriously
injured in an industrial accident. His mother spent several
days at the hospital while a neighbor watched the children. Peter knew something was terribly wrong, but "to
spare the children" he and his siblings were told few
details. When his father died, the children did not attend
the funeral. Whether this was to protect the children from
too much pain or to protect his mother from having to
take care of the children was not clear, but as a result of
not attending the funeral and not seeing his father in the
hospital, Peter never really had a chance to say good-bye.

After the funeral Peter remembers being told by relatives and family friends to be a "strong little man" and to
be "a good boy" who wouldn't cause his mother any problems and who would take care of his brother and sister.

Peter tried to take these injunctions quite seriously,
though he was suffering from intense grief himself. As a
nine-year-old child, his needs were great, yet he ignored
them to take care of the others, especially his mother, who
could no longer be the tower of emotional strength Peter
had come to expect. In this period of confusion, Peter felt
lost. Not only had he mysteriously lost his father, but his

mother had become emotionally unavailable, the family was in a financial crisis, and his siblings wouldn't heed him. He felt powerless and alone, yet he believed he was supposed to be strong and supportive.

When Peter entered therapy years later, he remembered little of these feelings. At age forty, all he knew was that his nine-year-old son was acting up, and Peter was furious with him. He had no control over him and could not talk to him. On his own Peter was not able to see the connections between what had happened to him as a boy and what was happening to him now as a father. Without realizing it, he had carried unexpressed grief over his father's sudden death with him for thirty-one years. As he began to face these issues, he recognized that his feelings of powerlessness in relation to his son were similar to the sense of powerlessness he had experienced as a nine-year-old in relation to his father's death. Then he had felt inadequate to take care of his mother and sister and brother. Now he felt inadequate to take care of his son. Then he had felt ashamed because he was angry at his father for dying. Now he felt ashamed because he lost his temper with his son.

Once Peter began to make these connections between his unresolved grief and his problem with his son, he was able to make the necessary changes. But first he had to talk about his father, visit his grave, cry over him, and finally be able to say good-bye to him. Until that process was completed, his grief came out as anger toward his son and toward himself.

A mother's death can be even more devastating. When a boy loses his mother, he loses the parent who is most likely his main source of emotional support. She is usually the person who helps the children through their emotional crises. In her absence a boy finds himself lost emotionally. Grieving for a lost mother is done without guidance. The person who was the boy's emotional guide is the one for whom he must now grieve. Many men who lost their mothers before adulthood never adequately mourned the loss. That early loss became a source of emotional discomfort throughout their lives, a wound that never healed, a void that was never filled.

My own father lost his mother, Rebecca, when he was six years old. Now a man in his seventies, my father can still recall the moment he was told of her death. She had been sick with influenza for many weeks. My father and his older brother were attending a movie. In the darkness of the movie theater they heard a cousin's voice calling their names. Startled and frightened, they left their seats and were informed that their mother had died.

In the aftermath, bitterness broke out in the family. Rebecca's family accused my father's father of not caring adequately for her. In the ensuing squabbles my father's needs were ignored. He was shuffled from one relative to another. His grieving was interrupted by his struggle to survive.

The consequences of this early loss were profound. Each year on Mother's Day for almost seventy years my father has visited her grave. He has also been dedicated to taking care of his wife's health needs no matter what the cost. He dreads making the mistake his father was accused of having made by his in-laws.

A few years ago I became aware of the consequences of not having mourned the loss of my maternal grandfather, who had committed suicide when I was twenty-three. After having put off cleaning the garage for months, I decided to confront the tangled extension cords, the dust-covered garden tools, and the boxes filled with items long forgotten and not missed but somehow too important to be thrown away.

Reluctantly I dug in. Not far into the sorting and tossing, I paused to examine the contents of a gray metal box. I was unprepared for my reaction as I discovered an old electric sander with a manila tag on it. I recognized it immediately as a pawn ticket from the shop where my grandfather had worked most of his life. In his beautiful handwriting I could still make out the words, "Henry Washington, June, 1958," the name of the man who had hocked the sander and the date it had to be claimed. Evidently Mr. Washington had not claimed it on time, so my grandfather had bought it cut-rate. Gazing at that ticket, I realized I had not seen anything in my grandfather's handwriting since his death in 1970.

I remembered myself, as a child, living with my parents and grandparents in a small suburban home, eagerly awaiting the return of Grandpa Izzie from the pawnshop on Saturday night. He would often bring home an array of drills, radios, and other unclaimed items. I always thought of them as his special gifts to me. Holding that ticket, I felt the rush of memories it summoned. It occurred to me that the small piece of cardboard was the only memento I still had of Izzie.

During the Detroit riots of 1967, the pawnshop was burned down. Less dramatically but just as inevitably, Izzie, out of work for the first time in his life, began deteriorating, too. For income he rekindled his old habit of gambling; as the losses mounted, his drinking increased. He began issuing suicide threats. I was teaching school in New York City when I received the call from my father. Izzie's final threat was not idle. He had killed himself by swallowing jeweler's acid, just as he had threatened many times before.

As I showed my wife and kids that tag, I felt myself fighting back the tears. In a way I wished they would finally flow. Due to the mixed feelings associated with his suicide, I had never been able to cry over the loss of my grandfather. The situation was made more complicated by the family's decision to keep the cause of death a secret. At his age, we figured why dishonor his memory? No one would doubt the family story that this heavy smoker had had a heart attack. Little did I understand that keeping the suicide a secret would block me from adequately mourning the grandfather I had loved so dearly. My friends knew my grandfather had died, but out of loyalty to my family I could share with no one my anguish over the manner of his death.

In the years immediately following his death my feelings about Izzie alternated between guilt and anger. As an only child growing up in a house of adults, my specialty had been to keep everyone cheerful, especially this alternately morose and exuberant man. I had failed to cheer him up this time. It seemed perfectly natural for me to major in psychology in college. As a psych student, moreover, shouldn't I have recognized the warning signs of suicide and been able to prevent it? Maybe if I hadn't left home he wouldn't have become so depressed. Maybe I should have invited him to visit me in New York City. The list of shoulds and maybes was long and persistent whenever I was reminded of Izzie, which happened often, since

I like to listen to Detroit Tiger baseball on the radio. Izzie always seemed to have a portable radio stuck in his ear, listening to Ernie Harwell, the voice of the Tigers. (Izzie liked to call them the Pussycats in those days of constant fifth-place finishes.)

The only match for my guilt was my anger. Somehow I could not easily forgive him for having tarnished two of my life's greatest joys. Izzie had always been my number one fan. How often I had heard him say, "Robbie, you're going to be a great man someday." With his encouragement I had made two important decisions in 1970: to apply to graduate school and to ask my girlfriend, Pat, to marry me. How sad and disappointed I felt that he had not waited around to hear about my acceptance at Harvard and to attend our wedding. If he had really cared about me, he would not have taken his life just four months before the wedding.

As the years went by, though, sorrow emerged as the dominant emotion. I missed him. I ached at the memory of him waking me up in the morning by imitating an alarm clock or driving me and my friends to high school in his '61 Chevy Nova. "Who's kicking me in the amplifier?" he'd ask the laughing teenagers in the backseat.

I was sad, too, that my own sons never had a chance to meet Izzie. They would have enjoyed this slight, handsome man who made bad jokes, spoke his own foreign tongue especially designed for his grandchildren, and who would pile all the kids in the neighborhood into his small car to take us to an afternoon Tigers game.

As I showed my sons the ticket, I was pleased that they, too, have wonderful relationships with their own grandfathers. I know, of course, that they were in no way responsible for their grandfathers' well-being. This thought helped me to realize that I wasn't to blame, and Izzie wasn't to be punished for taking his own life. Now I can understand how painful his undiagnosed manic-depression must have been. No, the most painful facet of Izzie's death — missing him — was simply a function of his passing away. Suicide and heart attacks have equal status there.

I detached the tag and gently cleaned off the dust. I realized that maybe a pawn ticket wasn't such an inappropriate memory for this man. In some ways he had pawned his own life away. But in many ways I owe a debt to him as well. He contributed much to who I am today: to the development of my playful side; to my courage to take risks; and to my love of baseball. Now I am determined not to allow his manner of death to obliterate the spirit of the man. To me he had been a hero, a dapper guy in a Fedora and a natty sport coat with his shoes always shined. As I placed the ticket in my wallet, I vowed never to stow it or his memory away again.

Your Own Experience with Grief

Grief occurs not only over death. Grief can be a reaction to almost any type of loss, and we have all experienced many. I invite you to reflect on your own losses and to ask yourself how adequately you have mourned these losses.

What does it mean to have mourned losses adequately? Of course, there is no one right way to grieve over a loss. It is a highly individualized process, and depends on the person grieving and the circumstances of the loss. However, there are certain characteristics that typify losses not adequately mourned. For example, from time to time do you replay in your mind the details of the loss? Or are you blocked from recalling the details? Did you feel inhibited about expressing your feelings? Were you ashamed of your feelings? Do you find yourself blocking the memory? Do you feel like your tears are locked somewhere in your body?

If you have adequately grieved over a loss, you can probably remember the details of the loss, you do recall having fully expressed your emotions over the loss (either at the time or subsequently), and you probably have cried over it. If you do experience flashbacks, they may be painful, but they do not necessarily overwhelm you and set off a deep depression.

In most cases people intuitively know whether or not they have adequately mourned a loss. Allow yourself some time now to think about and *feel* past losses in your life. Which ones still need some work in the grieving process? Don't neglect significant losses other than death or divorce, such as ending a relationship with a male friend (often these seem to fade away rather than to end abruptly as romantic relationships are more likely to do), losing a job, status, or full physical functioning (due to chronic health problems or permanent injury).

Grief can also be associated with a dysfunctional family. If your parents or siblings abused you, you have experienced a fundamental loss of trust. It has probably not been mourned because few people recognize it as a loss. Support groups like Alanon and Adult Children of Alcoholics offer a forum for adults to express grief over their families of origin. Participants grieve over childhoods lost to unpredictability, violence, selfishness, and chaos. When people in recovery programs talk about "healing their lost child," they are talking about a grieving process.

Today men face another type of loss, one that is subtle yet substantial. This is the loss of our concept of women solely as nurturing, self-sacrificing, stay-at-home wives who will be there to soothe our wounds, cook our meals, and raise our children while we go off to do battle in the workplace. It is the loss of woman as dear old mom who will always take care of us.

Men in midlife have witnessed monumental changes in society's concept of women. We explore men's reactions to these changes in detail in the next chapter, but I mention it here because the changes of the last few decades have been confusing and troubling to many men and may need grieving. Although some men have reacted supportively and others, angrily, I believe that feelings of loss underlie their reactions either way. With women's increased participation in the workplace, and the changes they have made in their views of men and their ideas about themselves as wives, they are no longer willing to play a strictly supportive role. This is mostly a healthy change for both men and women, but in this period of transition men's emotional responses are raw and confused. If men are able to grieve over the loss of the woman-as-mother ideal, perhaps we will be better able to accept, respect, and enjoy the "new woman."

Robert Bly wrote that "grief, rather than anger, is the doorway to a man's feelings." Our unresolved grief is probably the primary contributor to the deep sleep. To awaken we must revisit our grief. We must first go down into our souls and confront the emotional demons that we learned to repress so many years ago. Loss, if not adequately grieved, turns into anger. It is this anger that we explore in the next section.

Anger

Anger is probably the most acceptable emotion for men to express. Emotions whose expression is unacceptable — such as fear, jealousy, and sadness — we learn to channel into anger. Yet anger can be expressed only under very controlled circumstances. For example, we can express our anger toward those whom we perceive as having less status or authority than ourselves. But if we express it to those who have authority over us, we risk losing status, power, our jobs, or even our freedom.

To add to the confusion, if we do not express our anger when other men think we should, we also risk losing status. We'll be labeled a wimp, which is generally considered worse than being called a hothead.

Some men get in trouble because they are too quick to anger. A great many others have a hard time ever expressing their anger, even though they may report that they feel angry much of the time.

Scott remembers his father teasingly calling him names as a child. "Pluto was one of his favorites. He called me this because my ears drooped. He'd tease me about my looks, and he'd tease me about being lazy. But god forbid if I teased him back. I'd get so angry at him. If I'd display any type of anger toward him, he'd let me have it. But it was OK to get angry or to act aggressively toward my friends or even toward my younger brother. In fact, if I let the neighbor kids tease me, my dad would get angry at me. 'Don't let kids push you around,' he'd say, 'Show 'em you're the boss, that you're not afraid of them.'"

Scott's double bind illustrates a confusing complexity about men and anger. Failure to express anger through aggressive acts can be seen as a cardinal sin. If as young men we were being pushed around — either physically or psychologically — and we didn't stand up for ourselves, we were likely to be scorned by the other boys, teased, and questioned about our manhood. Not to express anger, if under the circumstances the peer group deems anger the appropriate response, is to risk being identified as something less than a man.

Yet to anger too quickly and too frequently is also inappropriate and can lead to rejection or scorn. No one feels comfortable around a man who is quick to lose his temper. Such a man is considered a "loose cannon" who might ignite at any time. He is too intimidating and too threatening to trust. His intimidating tactics may enable him to enjoy short-term success; but in the long run, those quick to anger tend to be rejected.

One of the most famous hotheads in recent history was Billy Martin. This flashy second baseman played for and managed numerous major league teams. At the beginning of each tenure with a new team, he was adored and admired for his feistiness. But after a year or two his angry outbursts at umpires, fans, players, and newspaper reporters became intolerable and got him fired. The fans had an ambivalent love affair with him. They loved his fiery temper — he was the type of guy who wouldn't take anything from anyone — but inevitably he went too far, and their love would turn to scorn.

Imploding and Hidden Rage. Men in the deep sleep do not usually express their anger as outrageously as Billy Martin. They are not men who tend to get into fistfights. But the way they manage their anger may be just as detrimental — to themselves and to their loved ones.

Imploding, or turning one's anger onto oneself, is a common and self-destructive way to manage anger. Imploding is getting angry at oneself. It is the voice of self-criticism harping at a variety of perceived shortcomings. It is the voice that says, "Nothing you do is good enough," that pounds the psyche with a chorus of self-doubt. It is the voice that questions decisions, criticizes choices, blames for failures, and downplays successes. It is the voice that saps energy, turns the blue skies gray, and tires the soul. In many men its name is depression.

Imploding often occurs in men who abhor outward displays of anger. Men who implode are frequently men who have learned that all outward displays of anger are bad, that showing one's anger in any form indicates lack of self-control and weakness. Typically such men grew up in households where displays of anger were simply not tolerated.

As these men look carefully at themselves and at their families of origin, they learn that they have lived under a myth. It is impossible for anyone to go through life without some outward displays of anger, although it can come out sideways, in disguised forms.

Mike described an example of implosion. It happened on a canoeing trip with his father and brother.

"After the first day of canoeing we gathered wood to make the campfire. As I started to pile the wood in the manner I am accustomed to, my brother Fred came over and told me there was a better way to do it. Immediately I felt angry, but I didn't say anything. I didn't want to upset the trip. So I let him show me his way. Before I knew it, it had become his fire. I just stood looking at him with my hands in my pockets. After a few minutes I was so angry, I just went off to my tent. I claimed I had a headache (which I did by this time) and just stayed there for the rest of the evening — angry alternately at Fred for butting in and at myself for being so accommodating and not standing up for myself."

Mike used the word *accommodating* to describe his behavior. This is frequently the way men who implode describe themselves. They view themselves as nice guys who go along with the wishes of others so as to avoid conflict, even if it means not standing up for what they believe in.

Mike knew how to build a fire but feared that if he challenged his brother's supposed helpfulness, his brother might get upset and conflict might ensue. He feared this conflict but was unsure why. Perhaps he feared rejection or couldn't bear the idea of his brother's anger at him. Or perhaps he feared his own anger. If he got into an argument with Fred, perhaps he would lose his own self-control by yelling or saying something stupid. Perhaps he'd end up looking foolishly out of control. In the group discussion about this incident, Mike explored all these possibilities. From discussing it, he learned how unhealthy it had been for him to turn his anger on himself. Nothing had been gained, and he developed a massive headache from it. Even though he avoided overt conflict, the others were upset with him for missing dinner.

The next time he vowed to do it differently. He would try to express directly that he was angry. He would try to say it in a straightforward manner. If he became upset while stating his anger, so be it. He had to learn to recognize that it was unreasonable to expect that he would never get angry.

In discussing the incident, Mike worried that if he let his anger show, he might not be able to get it back under control. "I fear that if I start, I might not be able to stop. I might lose my temper and hurt somebody."

Mike then saw that this fear of his temper related to his upbringing. His father lost his temper frequently; and when he did, it was dangerous for Mike and his entire family. His father would scream, ridicule, and often hit Mike, his brothers, and his mother. As a young man Mike had vowed that he would not be like his father. No matter what happened, he would not allow himself to lose his temper.

For years he had been successful at controlling his anger. But, as is so often the case, Mike had overcorrected. Not only had he controlled his temper, but he had not allowed for any expression of his anger. Instead he had disciplined himself to keep under control at all times. Instead of finding a middle ground — a way to express his anger verbally but not go out of control with it — he had suppressed it altogether. For Mike the challenge was to find balance, to find a safe way to express anger without having to fear losing control like his father.

Men like Mike, who strive so valiantly to keep their anger under control, find that their anger expresses itself in some hidden or unexpected ways. While on the surface they seem in control of anger, they experience other problems that may be related to their suppression of anger. Some of the most common indirect expressions of anger are excessive sarcasm, cynical or flippant conversation, and constant putdowns. Even though offered in the guise of humor, comments or jokes from such men sting and can leave the recipient hurt.

Clay was a man with this style of communication. On the surface he always appeared happy-go-lucky, but in his men's group he always entered with a greeting that contained mixed elements of humor and sarcasm. The recipient inevitably felt confused: Was Clay being friendly or hostile? At one meeting, for example, Clay greeted Terry, who owned a clothing store, with a comment about how he had stopped by the store only to find that they didn't have a shirt he wanted in his size. "Hey, Terry," Clay said, "you sure have a beautiful selection of shirts in your store. I just wish you'd carry them in my size." Terry, feeling put down by this remark, decided to try to get clarification from Clay.

"Clay, you sound angry about that!"

Clay quickly denied any anger. "No, Terry, just teasing. You have the nicest store in town."

But Terry's comment had opened up the floodgates. The other group members also began to confront Clay about his sarcasm. Each remembered remarks that he had made to them that made them feel confused or put down. At first Clay denied that any hostility was intended, but as the group continued to question him, he recognized that this sarcastic style of conversation was his way of channeling his anger.

"In my family," Clay finally revealed, "no direct expression of anger was allowed. If I yelled, swore, or threw something, I was severely reprimanded. I knew if I got into a fistfight I'd be punished. So I guess I learned to use my humor as a way to defend myself. I became the put-down king. I was macho from the neck up. I guess I don't usually think of myself as angry and hostile, but maybe I am. Maybe that's why I seem to alienate people who are close to me."

Hidden anger can take many other forms besides sarcasm. Among the most common are

1. Procrastination or habitual lateness
2. Excessive cheerfulness, politeness, or obsequiousness
3. Chronic fatigue or depression
4. Psychosomatic disorders, including ulcers, tics, or excessive concern and worry about health issues
5. Self-destructive behaviors, such as smoking, picking at self (nose, sores), excessive risk taking (driving while drinking, driving too fast)

Raging Men. Not all men in the deep sleep suppress their anger. There are many men, like Billy Martin, who are outwardly and chronically angry and who resort to rage and aggression as an expression of their anger. These are the men who appear ready to fly off the handle at any time. Their wives and children fear them because of this uncontrollable rage. Typically these men have been raised in an excessively punitive atmosphere, where one or both of their parents frequently lost control of their temper. However, unlike Mike, who compensated by suppressing all outward manifestations of anger, these men have modeled themselves after the irate parent.

Such men usually come into therapy because their angry outbursts have got them into trouble. Typically they have been reported to protective services for abusing a child or have been arrested for spouse abuse. For such men psychotherapeutic treatment is necessary. They must learn how harmful (and illegal) such angry outbursts are.

They also have to learn new ways of relating that are not based on domination, intimidation, or coercion. If not treated adequately and correctly, such men can be serious threats to their families and to society. Men who turn their anger into violence are responsible for many of the severe problems we face in our society, including child abuse, domestic violence, and violent crimes outside of the family.

I do not intend to imply that all acts of domestic violence are committed by men. Women (and children) lose their tempers, too. Women sometimes hit men. But the vast majority of acts of domestic violence involve men hurting women and children. We need to accept this fact and grapple with its implications for our relationships with women and children.

Suggestions for Better Understanding Your Anger

1. Begin by keeping track of your patterns of anger. Write down either in a notebook or on index cards events or circumstances that made you angry during the course of a day. If you see yourself as the type of person who has difficulty expressing or even recognizing anger, record events that you think should have made you angry. Record the event itself, your reaction to the event, and the aftermath or consequences of the event.

The following is an example from Arnie:

Event: I was out visiting my mother, who was sick. When I came home, I went to take a nap because I was exhausted. When I woke up, my wife was upset with me because I had not pitched in to help make dinner.

My reaction: I got angry at her because I thought it was unfair that she would be mad at me for taking a nap. I had a difficult time with my mother, and my wife should have been more sympathetic to me.

Consequences: I helped out and didn't say anything but was angry at my wife all evening.

2. After tracking your anger for a week, review the journal. Can you find any patterns? Did you have more or fewer angry experiences than you would have supposed? Have you had difficulty recognizing or identifying your anger? How do you feel about the way you handled anger? How would you like to make improvements in the way you handle anger?

3. Seek out someone you trust and share the anger journal with that person. This may be the hardest part. At first it is too threatening for many people. But it is a crucial step. To improve on the way you handle anger, it helps to get feedback from others. Ask how they see you handling anger. Do they agree with your perceptions of how you express (or don't express) anger? What changes do they wish you would make in how you deal with anger?

If you can think of no one with whom to share your anger journal, you may want to consider finding a men's group or a professional counselor who will listen to these intimate reflections.

4. Based on your anger journal, formulate goals for improving the way you handle anger. These goals might be something like, "I need to learn to express anger in words rather than acts; to learn to say that I am angry rather than to slam doors, stomp my feet or throw things," or "I need to begin to acknowledge to myself that I really am angry at times. I'm not just frustrated, I'm furious, and I need to admit it."

Here are some other examples of goals: "I need to find ways to calm down when I get angry. I have choices: I can walk away, breathe deeply, take a walk, work in the garden"; "I have a right to my anger. It's not always my fault when my wife or children are upset. Sometimes they are wrong, too. I don't need to hurt or intimidate anyone, but I do have a right to my anger"; "I must avoid personally attacking others when I feel angry. It does me and my loved ones no good when I shout at them or shake my fist at them. I need to learn to control my temper"; "I need to avoid drinking. When I drink, my anger gets ugly. I say and do things I regret"; "Rather than blaming others for my anger, I need to learn to accept responsibility for it."

The men I have worked with have been able to make significant changes once they recognize their anger, determine to improve, and, most important, share their goals with their loved ones.

5. *Once the goals are established, it is crucial to continue to keep the anger journal.*   To monitor progress you need to keep track of anger patterns for an extended period. Our patterns of anger have been learned and reinforced for many years. If you resolve to change them, you must expect change to occur gradually. Learning to be more attuned to feelings is like beginning a new exercise regime. You cannot expect to run a marathon immediately. You need to build up your emotional strength gradually, just as you would your muscles.

GUIDELINES FOR BECOMING MORE IN TOUCH
WITH OUR FEELINGS

So far in this chapter I have emphasized the importance of gaining awareness of two key emotions for men, grief and anger. Of course these are just two of the myriad emotions we experience daily. Now I offer some general guidelines on how to "get in touch with your feelings." This phrase is used so often to describe what men need to do with their lives that it has become a cliche. Yet it applies to most of the men I meet, especially the ones who enter therapy or who are having difficulty with relationships. One of the men I work with said the idea of getting in touch with feelings reminded him of a line from a song by Bob Seger, "working on mysteries without any clues." The more I thought about it, the more this line rang true. Many men do not have a clue as to how to better understand their emotional sides. Here are some clues to the mystery.

Step 1. Learn to recognize when you are experiencing a feeling. At a very basic level we must first become aware of what an emotion feels like. To do this we must become aware of bodily sensations, because emotions are first and foremost bodily sensations. Sweaty palms, a racing heart, discomfort in the pit of the stomach, a choking sensation, pain or tightness in the chest, and tingling in the fingers are among the many physical signs that denote feelings. As men we have been taught to ignore such signs or to see them as signs of weakness. To learn to recognize feelings means to go against this male mandate and to begin to accept bodily sensations as indicators of emotions. These sensations are as ever present as birds in the woods on a summer day. Just as we can be unaware of the birds until someone points them out or until one flies close to us, we can easily be unaware of the presence of feelings. We need to learn to listen to our bodies with an inner focus, a sustained concentration. We need to allow ourselves to slow down and heed the signals our body sends us.

So, too, with our thoughts. Emotions have a cognitive component as well as a physical one. We need to allow ourselves quiet, reflective time to listen to our inner thoughts. How are we reacting to situations? What is our inner dialogue? We need to tune in to that dialogue. Part of us is reacting one way, part another. If we concentrate we can learn to distinguish between our own inner voices.

Many men have found journals to be an effective tool for becoming better attuned to sensations and thoughts. Create your own format. There is no one correct way to keep a journal. Just try to concentrate on recording what you are feeling from day to day. If you do want to keep a journal, allot time on a daily basis simply to sit and allow yourself to feel.

Step 2. Identify the feeling. Once we have become aware that we are experiencing a feeling, we need to learn to distinguish one feeling from another. Most men don't have an emotional vocabulary. At first we are overwhelmed to learn that there are hundreds of words and phrases for emotions. Many of us feel like the white explorer who is astonished to discover that Eskimos have hundreds of words for snow. But just as the Eskimos need to distinguish between the varieties of snow to be able to survive, we need to distinguish between our feelings to be able to grow as men.

In your journal try to name the feeling you are experiencing. Practice using metaphors to describe your feelings, for example, "I feel like a new moon rising," or "I feel like algae in a lake." Let your creative mind take over. Write down whatever metaphor comes into your mind. It may be a reference to nature, to history ("I feel like Napoleon at Waterloo"), to movies or plays ("I feel like Paul Newman in *Cool Hand Luke*), to sports ("I feel like Jimmy Connors when he got to the semifinals at the U.S. Open at age thirty-nine"), or to any association that your creative mind finds.

Step 3. Identify what has triggered the feeling. Once we realize that we are experiencing a feeling, and once we can recognize what that feeling is, we need to be able to understand the link between the particular feeling and the events that may have elicited it. Sometimes the triggering event is obvious — an upsetting argument with one's wife or failure to get a promotion. But at other times finding the roots of our feelings is far more subtle or confusing. We wake up in a bad mood and don't know why. We are having a pleasant time when seemingly out of the blue we begin to worry about something apparently unrelated to our current circumstances.

Often we are confused because we are having a delayed emotional reaction. Because we have trained ourselves not to react emotionally, we may not experience our feelings at the moment of an upsetting event. Several hours or even days after, we find ourselves upset. Our anger may be triggered by something trivial — a traffic delay or a child not following through on a chore. When we find ourselves overreacting, we need to ask ourselves if something else is bothering us. It may be something major, such as a health worry or insecurity about a job occasioned by a remark from the boss. Rather than dealing with the upsetting event, we disciplined ourselves to put it out of our minds. We thought we were successful, but if we look closely, our bad mood or loss of temper was probably triggered by a delayed reaction to this problem. As we learn to better understand and record our feelings, we need to monitor the relationship between our immediate feelings, the overriding stresses in our lives, and the unresolved feelings from the past we may be carrying with us.

Step 4. Communicate about your feelings to others.   In my opinion this is the most crucial step in the process of learning to become better attuned to feelings. It is also often the most difficult. It is learning to acknowledge vulnerability. It is learning to be honest and open with our feelings not only with ourselves but with others. It is the step that most goes against the grain of everything we have learned about being a man.

There is nothing complicated in the how-to of this step. It is just a matter of doing it. Certainly you should begin with those people you trust the most. Sharing your feelings with friends is the best way to practice expressing feelings.

The reason this step is so crucial is that through sharing feelings with others, you get feedback on how they experience you and how they themselves are feeling. One of the most common responses I get from men in the men's groups is surprise at how liberating and satisfying it is to talk honestly about feelings to other men. Many men are relieved to learn, often for the first time, that they are not alone in their feelings. Feelings they had concealed for so many years are no different from the feelings of others. Admitting this gives them strength rather than making them appear weak, as they had feared.

Step 5. Identify your needs based on your feelings. Once you begin to acknowledge your feelings, you begin to truly understand your needs. A major consequence of hiding our feelings from ourselves and others is a lack of clarity about our true needs. If we don't know how we feel, we can't know what we need. Instead of pursuing our true needs, we have pursued those markers of success that society deems important. Once we begin to acknowledge and share our feelings, we may radically redefine our needs. If we identify that we are feeling lonely, for example, we can see that we need more friendships. If we identify that we are feeling anxious much of the time, we can see that we need more tranquility. If we feel jealous of our wives' attention to the children, we can see that we need more affection.

Once we are clearer about our needs, we can begin to formulate goals that more truly reflect who we are and who we want to be as people. Our goals will then be based on who we are as unique human beings rather than on what society says we need. As you focus on your feelings or record them in a journal, ask yourself on a regular basis what you need. I am not talking about writing a to-do list of tasks. I am referring to needs such as companionship, love, self-care, rest, and excitement. If you can learn to identify needs, your to-do lists will become different. Instead of just focusing on what has to get done, you will begin to consider what will make you feel better, such as taking a walk, finding quiet time, or calling a friend.

In review, the five steps for getting in better touch with our emotions are to

1. Recognize when you are experiencing a feeling.

2. Identify the feeling.

3. Identify what has triggered the feeling.

4. Communicate your feelings to others.

5. Identify your needs based on your feelings.

In order to follow these steps, it is useful to develop a daily practice using some of the following techniques:

- Keeping a journal. Each day at a regular time (either early morning or late evening) record in your journal how you are feeling. You can use the preceding five steps, or you can devise your own to try to tap in to your prevailing emotional state on a daily basis.

- Talking with others. Set up a regular time to talk to someone you trust about your feelings. This could be a significant other, a friend, a therapist, or members of a counseling or self-help group.

- Prayer. Many men set up a regular time for spiritual reflection, which includes a time for reflection on feelings.

- Spontaneous reflections. Keep a journal or index cards on hand to write down feelings at the time you are experiencing them. This helps you reflect on your feelings at the moment you are most aware of them.

- Artistic experiences. Open yourself to respond emotionally to music, movies, TV, poetry, stories, and natural beauty. If you find yourself becoming emotional listening to an old song, or tearing up during a movie, reflect on the experience. Try to be attuned to the roots of the emotion.

- Inspirational reading. Read emotionally inspiring material on a daily basis. Many excellent books of daily meditations are now available. One, entitled *Touchstones* (Harper/Hazeldon), is specifically written for men. As you read, allow yourself to reflect on your reactions, perhaps in your journal.

- Making art. Try to gain access to your feelings through some form of artistic expression. Painting, sculpting, and photography are some of the ways people express their feelings.

Just as we are surrounded by the natural environment, we are afloat in the world of emotion. It is ever-present. Awakening to emotion is as basic as opening our senses to nature. Only instead of turning our senses outward, we turn them inward. If we can look inward without fear, our inner panorama may be as beautiful and startling as the ocean and the mountains.

5 WAKING UP TO WOMEN

Randy was a new member of the group. He began his first session with a desperate plea. "Guys, I need some help. My wife says unless I change, she wants a divorce. She says I don't communicate with her, but I'm trying as hard as I can. I'm confused. No matter what I do it doesn't seem good enough for her. I don't even know what I'm supposed to do anymore. I keep trying to be a good husband, a good father, to provide as best I can for the family, but I guess I just keep screwing up."

Phil was sympathetic. "I know how you feel. My mood seems to go up and down, depending on my wife's mood. When she tells me she loves me, when she treats me nice, I feel good. A few nice words, some good sex, and I'm happy. But when she criticizes me, I can't take it. I'm doing the best I can, but she just doesn't seem to appreciate how hard I'm trying."

Derrick, too, related to Randy's situation. "When my wife is upset with me, I feel terrible. I can't stand having her upset with me. If she gets real upset, I'll do whatever I can to get her out of that mood. I don't always agree with what she wants me to do, but if she asks, I'll do it. Trouble is, she doesn't always ask. Sometimes I have to guess at what she wants. Ever since I was a kid that's how I survived. I figured what people wanted and then acted accordingly. But now my wife wants me to say what I want for myself, and I haven't a clue. It's like she's asking me to program a computer, but I don't have any computer skills."

Two other men in our group, Mike and Arnie, weren't so eager to continue to please their partners. They had become fed up with being the sole support of their mates. "I feel like a guy walking around carrying a pyramid," said Mike. Each year someone would add another block to it. First it was marriage. Then a job. Then a child. A better job. A bigger home. A second job. It got to the point where I dreaded getting up each day, there'd be so much weight to carry around. By the time I got home at around 8:30 at night, I was exhausted. I didn't feel like talking to my wife. I just wanted my food, my newspaper, and my bed."

Arnie, the physician, agreed. "I've been working since I was twelve. I put myself through college and graduate school. When I married, I thought nothing of working long hours. But now I feel like a mule. Every morning I get up and put on the harness. True, I'm not plowing the fields, but when you see so many problems day after day, it can feel like a real burden. At least at work the staff treats me well. But when I get home, I feel that she doesn't appreciate me. She just puts more demands on me. I feel like one of those automatic bank machines — just push my buttons and out comes the money."

Scott seemed to be getting upset with Randy. "It sounds to me like you let her push you around too much. I think a man needs to be firmer with a woman. They expect us to be stronger, even though they say they don't. If you try so hard to please her, she's just going to expect more from you. You're going to drive yourself crazy. You need to decide what you want for yourself, take a strong stand, and stick to it. She'll come around."

The group had expressed some common themes that men invariably replay when we talk about relationships with women. These can be summarized as follows:

As men we expect a lot from the significant woman in our lives. Most of us count on one woman to be our best friend, our exclusive lover, the mother of our children, our main source of emotional support, our social planner, our liaison with our families of origin, and manager of the details of family life. Furthermore, even though we may share some household tasks, we probably count on this same woman to be the chief executive officer for cleaning, cooking, and parenting.

Our expectations of women derive from the beliefs of an era that is rapidly fading. No longer can we expect to marry a gal just like the gal who married dear old dad. Women have changed. They now want a marital arrangement that is more egalitarian, with better communication. Women have woken up to their rights and are calling upon men to shed some of our power.

Even if we are sympathetic with women's concerns, we are confused and hurt that many women today see us as the cause of their pain. We have tried to accept the responsibilities taught us in our youth: to be a good provider; to protect women; to be a loving father; to be strong and determined. Most of us have never intentionally hurt or suppressed women.

As women have begun to demand their rights, much of what we have been taught about relationships has become obsolete. Yet no new model has emerged to take the place of the one being rejected.

This is the challenge we face today: To understand what women want; to figure out what we want, and to forge a new balanced model of male-female relationships that can meet both of our needs as well as the needs of our children.

In this chapter we explore the social and emotional aspects of our relationships with women. In the next, the focus is on our sexual relationships.

OBSTACLES TO CHANGE

Three major obstacles stand in the way of our developing more mutually satisfying relationships with women: (1) we have been raised to work, not to relate; (2) we have learned from our parents patterns of relating to women that no longer work; and (3) we have not learned to appreciate some basic differences in the way men and women are taught to relate. We'll explore these obstacles one at a time.

Obstacle 1: We have been raised to work, not to relate

As men we have been raised to be effective in the workplace. Unfortunately the competitive values emphasized at work are usually not compatible with the cooperative skills necessary to function effectively in intimate relationships.

When they first marry, men are usually attentive and alive in the relationship. But over the years a destructive pattern emerges. At first the husband defines his primary masculine role as that of provider for the family. With his emphasis on work, he has little time for his friends or his extended family. His wife becomes his social and emotional lifeline, though increasingly he has difficulty giving emotionally. His orientation is toward competition, not relationships; his language is that of work, not of love.

When they have children, he feels even more pressure to be a good provider. Even if his wife works, the husband typically still feels more responsibility for supporting the family. He believes he is showing love and devotion by being a good provider, but his wife experiences him as inattentive, preoccupied, and uninterested in the family. She complains that he is more interested in his career than in her.

Because he works in a competitive world, he is unsure of himself. He therefore craves reassurance from his wife. He wants to know that he is special to her and that his efforts are appreciated. He measures his reassurance by her attentiveness to him. In addition to her emotional support, he counts on her sexual attention as a sign of affirmation.

She may complain not only about his apparent indifference to family life but also about her unequal share of household duties. Research shows that even in the 1990s, the husband does considerably less housework and child care than the wife. Even when they have jobs outside the home, most wives do approximately fifteen hours more housework each week than their husbands. Over a year this adds up to an extra month of twenty-four-hour days. This often leads to resentment on the part of the woman (Arlie Hochschild *The Second Shift* [New York: Avon Books, 1989]).

Eventually the man begins to resent his wife's complaints, feeling that his efforts to provide are unappreciated. While he may be sympathetic to his wife's request that he spend more time at home or with the children, he begins to believe that she has no sympathy for how hard he is trying or how pressure-packed his work is or how exhausted he is when he finally returns home.

In a bitter dance of resentment, he feels she is trying to fence him in, and she feels he is trying to escape, to distance himself from her. He feels she is nagging, making unfair demands on him. She feels he won't listen to her. Each believes the other is insensitive to his or her needs. If the situation persists and the couple is unable to talk through their differences, each partner grows angrier.

Meanwhile the woman may be changing. She may start to challenge the tenets of the feminine code. This code, which is well described in the book *Too Good for Her Own Good* (Bepko and Krestin [New York: HarperCollins, 1990]), includes these implicit rules for women: be attractive, be a lady, be unselfish and of service, make relationships work, and be competent without complaint. For a man raised in the post–World War II baby-boom generation, the implicit bargain was that if he followed the male code (be a good provider, be strong, honest, independent), he would marry a woman who followed the female code and they would live happily ever after. This, of course, has rarely been true.

Even though intellectually the husband may agree with many feminist principles, he is bewildered when confronted with change. His wife is not there for him in the way he had come to expect. She may have found a job or gone back to school, or, if she has already been working outside the home, she may become more invested in her job or begin to pursue new interests outside the home. She may decide to try self-help courses, a Twelve-Step group, or counseling. She may even pressure him to do likewise.

Most men in such circumstances feel not like a villain but a victim. They don't understand what has happened. A man who enters therapy in response to the fear of losing his wife usually feels emotionally shaken, like Rip Van Winkle suddenly awakened out of a deep emotional sleep. He does not realize how his adherence to the male code—

competitiveness, keeping score, and following the rules of
the game— has led him to the precipice of disaster.

Obstacle 2: We adhere to outmoded patterns of relating to women, which we learned from our parents

A man's attitude toward his mate is almost always a reflection of the model of male-female relationships he
observed in his family of origin. Even though intellectually he may not agree with the model, if he does not completely understand and has not dealt with his feelings
about it, he may repeat it. Men who have not come to
terms with their fathers especially risk inadvertently mir-
roring the father's behavior.

The three predominant maladaptive patterns of relating to women are (1) men who try to please their wives too
much; (2) men who are emotionally withdrawn; and (3)
men who use coercion or domination to control their wives.

People-pleasing Men.   These are men who have grown
up with the notion that the best way to survive is to find a
woman and then do whatever is needed to make her
happy. Their creed is as follows: Anticipate her needs and
try to fulfill them; avoid conflict because it might lead to
her rejection of you; derive a sense of well-being from the
security of being loved. They accommodate her needs
even if it means not always getting what they want. If she
has a problem, they fix it. If she is unhappy, they make her
happy. Whatever happens, don't let go of her. She is life,
an emotional iron lung.

Generally men in the excessive people-pleasing mode
are not proud of it. They tend to be ashamed because it

does not conform to the strong, independent image of a "real man." We learn as young men that no man should constantly accommodate his wife's needs. A real man stands up and takes control in a relationship with a woman. Excessively accommodating men are described as "pussy-whipped," henpecked, or soft.

Pleasing one's wife is not always wrong, of course. In fact, acting excessively strong and independent in a marriage is a blueprint for disaster. Healthy women do not want to be dominated. The problem is that a person who constantly goes to extremes to please a partner loses his or her self in the process.

Robin Norwood, in her best-selling book *Women Who Love Too Much* (Los Angeles: Jeremy Tarcher, 1985), describes this pattern in women. My clinical experience indicates that this similar pattern exists in men as well. These are the characteristics of a man in the people-pleasing mode:

- His primary orientation to life is the seeking of approval of his spouse.

- To gain approval he constantly accommodates himself to his spouse's wishes and needs.

- He has difficulty knowing how he feels, so he relies on his wife's feedback to measure his own emotional state.

- His feelings about himself are tied to how his wife feels about him.

- He avoids conflict, which he fears may lead to her withdrawal of love.

- Although he feels responsible for taking care of the needs of everyone in the family, he has difficulty recognizing his own needs.

- He fears losing his wife's love or earning her disapproval.

- He is periodically depressed, feeling guilty about not trying hard enough.

- He is periodically angry at his spouse because she doesn't appreciate his efforts.

- He has difficulty expressing this anger directly.

Men who adopt the people-pleasing mode were typically raised in families where they played a primary caretaking role at an early age. They either modeled themselves on fathers who were people pleasing and submissive or served as substitute husbands for absent or emotionally distant fathers. At a relatively early age a boy in these circumstances learned to get the approval of his mother by being attentive to her and learning how to please her. Often these were families where the mother was disappointed in or angry at the father. The son learned that if he could be different from his father, he could gain his mother's approval. His efforts to please mother set up a conflict: To please mother he had to be different from father, but his father would not approve of him if he was too much of a mama's boy. So the son learned to display two sides of himself. When he was with his mother, he was responsive and caring. When he was with his father (and perhaps his peers), he was competitive and aggressive. This pattern is maintained in adulthood. When he is out with the boys, he may be macho; but when he is at home, he does whatever is necessary to please his wife.

John was typical of such men. His idea of being a loving father was to be a great provider for his wife and children. By being competitive, disciplined, and learning the politics of the corporation, he was able to earn lots of money, which for him was the mark of success.

But his wife had not married him for his money. She wanted his company, his partnership. She wanted him to share more of himself, not just his paycheck. He wanted to please, but he felt trapped between her needs and the demands of the corporation.

Gradually their relationship deteriorated. John felt trapped. It seemed the harder he worked, the deeper in debt he became. By constantly trying to provide the finest for his family, he became more enslaved to having to earn big money. The more he had to work, the less he felt in harmony with his wife. It was a cycle he could not stop. By the time John entered therapy, his marriage was nearly in ruins, he was exhausted physically and mentally, and he could see no way out.

Emotionally Withdrawn Men.   Throughout this book I have presented many examples of this type of man, who out of a fundamental difficulty in relationship to women tends to bury himself in work and outside activities, thereby avoiding intimate contact with women. The characteristics of the emotionally withdrawn man are

- His primary orientation to life is seeking success in the workplace or in competitive activities.

- He lives a dual life — at work alive and active; at home listless, disengaged, preoccupied.

- He appears self-centered, more focused on taking care of his own needs than specific needs of family members.

- He defines his contribution to the family as bringing home the paycheck and enabling family members to live comfortably.

- He resents his wife's demands that he be more available emotionally.

- He complains often of feeling tired or of having physical ailments.

- He either does not want children at all or is emotionally distant from them.

- He is uncomfortable with the language of intimacy: talking about feelings, being sensitive to others' needs; being attentive to small details that make his mate feel good.

- He tends to view his own neediness as a weakness.

The emotionally distant man typically grew up with a father who himself was emotionally distant. Often his mother was also emotionally unavailable due to the excessive demands placed on her by family responsibilities. Many of these men were raised in families where one or both of the parents were alcoholic. In such families these men never learned the subtleties of intimacy. They usually did not receive the type of close care and attention that would lead to a sense of security. As children they were likely to be emotionally neglected by parents. A surprising number of them also lost a parent at an early age, either through death, divorce, or abandonment.

Mike is an example of an emotionally distant man. Mike came into therapy distraught because his daughter had been diagnosed with a chronic, debilitating illness. For most of his life he had devoted himself to his career as a carpenter and to providing for his family. He had been with the same company for twenty-one years. Most days he got up early, worked on the job till seven, came home, ate the dinner his wife had made. Then he worked on odd jobs, watched TV (with or without her), flossed, brushed, and went to bed. For many years his routine rarely varied.

As he sat in the chair in my office he seemed perplexed. He thought his path had been set for life: work hard, save, put the children through school, retire early, and spend the last years of life traveling and pursuing hobbies. Why was he feeling so strange? He had no idea how to relate to his daughter in her debilitated condition. He was scared, but he had no language to use to connect with his daughter.

Mike's orientation to life was to work hard and be responsible. This left him no time (nor inclination) to focus on relationships and emotional needs. He would provide for his family through hard work, just like his father. If this meant he wasn't close to people, so be it. But now he realized how important connectedness with loved ones was in his life. While his daughter's illness was devastating to him and his family, it was the crisis that awakened him to the parts of himself that had been numbed from the years of excessive focus on work and success.

Might Makes Right.   The third category of men we see in problematic relationships with women are those who regularly use power tactics to dominate and control the relationship. To a certain extent, all relationships between men and women involve power struggles. However, the particular pattern that I describe here goes beyond typical power struggles to include the regular use of coercion or force to get one's way.

Perhaps nothing is more difficult for a therapist than confronting a man whose wife accuses him of using force and even violence in a relationship. Yet I have found over the years that opening the door on this topic can often have a positive impact on men. At a certain level they are aware of what they are doing and that it is wrong. What they do not know are any alternatives.

Men who use dominance and power in marriage or with their children usually experienced it themselves when they were growing up. They resented it then but were powerless to do anything about it. Many of them saw their fathers use force against their mothers and consider themselves abused children. They know it was wrong of their fathers, and they sense it is wrong for themselves, but it is the only way they know to behave in a relationship. Feeling powerless to do anything else, they resort to force. When confronted, at first they may deny it and get angry; but eventually they are thankful for being confronted. Almost always they are eager to learn new ways of relating.

In discussing men who use dominance and control in a relationship, I am describing a wide range of behavior, including subtle forms of control, such as belittling and condescension, as well as more overt forms, such as threatening or actually using physical violence. But more than specific behaviors, I am describing a certain attitude toward women. It is the attitude that says that men are superior to women and should be in control of the relationship because of this superiority. As has been well-documented, society has fed this belief. "Men are rational, women, emotional"; "men are courageous, women, fearful"; "Times of crisis call for a man's cool head"; "She really wants it, she just can't let herself admit it"; "Men have superior intelligence, especially in the hard sciences"; "Because women are weaker, we need to protect them."

In her best-selling book *Backlash: The Undeclared War Against American Women* (New York: Crown Publishers, 1991), the journalist Susan Faludi documents how pervasive the negative stereotypes of women remain in our society, even after twenty-five years of the modern women's movement. Faludi enumerates some of these myths: that working women are unhappier; that they can't find husbands; and that they are more often infertile. Faludi believes the perpetuation of these ideas is an attempt to keep women "in their place."

"Keeping women in their place" leads to dire consequences for many women. According to a recent paper on the topic, "At least one in six women in the United States is abused each year by her mate. Between 18 and 36% of women are physically abused by a male partner at some time in their lives. Severe repeated violence occurs in one in 14 marriages. During the Viet Nam War, from 1967 — 1973 the U.S. lost 39,000 soldiers. During the same period, almost half that number, 17,500 of American women and children, were killed by family members" (J. M. Avis, "Where Are All the Family Therapists?" *Journal of Marital and Family Therapy* 18, 3 [April 1992]).

Most men who read these statistics can readily say,
"That is terrible, but it is not me." Yet on a milder scale,
the need for control that a man feels in relationship to a
woman may result in subtle but still damaging behaviors
in the home, including

- ignoring his mate's opinions because she is not sufficiently "informed" or "rational";
- trying to put her or her family down through comments, ridicule, or hostile looks;
- not helping out with the housework or child care
  because it is "women's work";
- preventing her from getting or keeping a job;
- allowing her no input in important decisions, especially financial ones;
- smashing, kicking, or destroying things;
- persisting with sexual demands when she is not
  receptive, or making her feel guilty or inadequate;
- enlisting the children in affirming his point of view
  against her;
- denying the abuse or blaming her for it.

Men who use dominance to control relationships are
usually highly competitive men who see the world, even
relationships, in hierarchical, win-lose terms. In some
cases, an abusive man believes this is what his wife wants.
If he fails to dominate her, he believes she will see him as
less than a man.

One rarely finds a man — or a woman, for that matter
— who has never displayed at least some of these behaviors. Nonetheless a relationship based on control through

physical or emotional abuse cannot be a healthy relationship. Because the patterns are so deeply engrained, very few couples or individuals are able to change without outside help. If you see yourself in this portrait of the domineering man, I strongly encourage you to seek professional help.

The patterns of relating to women that I have described are not necessarily static. During the course of a relationship a man can cycle through all three. One of my clients illustrates the cyclical nature of these patterns in some men.

Lou, a forty-seven-year-old teacher, has been married for twenty-five years to Sylvia, a branch manager of a bank. They have a nineteen-year-old son in college and a seventeen-year-old son in high school. Lou is from a working-class family. His mother was a competent woman who had to drop out of high school due to the economic pressures of the Depression. His father was an auto worker who put in long hours and had a fierce temper that kept everyone in the family on edge.

Because Lou was the eldest child, he became his mother's confidante and companion. His mother catered to his dad to keep him from getting angry with the children, who made it a point to stay out of his way.

Much of Lou's motivation to be an excellent student derived from his desire to please his mother, an intelligent woman who was ashamed that she had never gotten her high school degree. Though her job as a waitress was necessary to supplement her husband's meager income, she found it humiliating.

In college Lou met Sylvia, who was from a stable middle-class family in New York. He fell madly in love with her and her family, which had the refinement and sophistication his family lacked. Though Sylvia was not initially interested in Lou, he pursued her with persistence and charm. By the time Lou earned his undergraduate degree, he had convinced Sylvia to marry him.

Lou devoted himself to Sylvia, and the early years of the marriage were a joy. They traveled extensively and were able to buy a new house. The real tension did not appear for six years, until they had children, which Lou really did not want in the first place. He was afraid he would display the same type of temper with his children as his father had with him. But to make Sylvia happy, Lou had acquiesced. At first he was delighted with Brad, but after a few months he found himself increasingly jealous of Sylvia's devotion to their son. About a year later he relented once again when Sylvia wanted to have a second child. With two children and a wife to support, Lou began to work extra jobs: he managed the yearbook, helped coach the track team, and taught driver's training in the summer. His patience with the children grew thin; on several occasions he lost his temper completely and hit Brad.

When Sylvia threatened to leave unless he changed, the couple entered counseling. Lou was shocked to discover that he had begun to repeat his family pattern: He had become a distant, mean father, and his wife and sons were closer to each other than he was to any of them.

Lou vowed to do whatever was necessary to win back his wife. She wanted him to be home more; he agreed to stop the extra work. She wanted to go back to work; he would support her. She wanted him to share his feelings more often and deeply. He promised to do anything to save the marriage. But as the children grew older and Sylvia's career prospered, she was less available to him. He tried to be supportive, but he found himself angry with her and then upset with himself at his anger. Although he was devoted to his children, he had difficulty feeling close to them. He had enjoyed fishing and hunting, but he gave up these interests because his wife did not approve.

By the time he reentered therapy at age forty-seven, he was an unhappy, embittered man with few friends. In the classroom he had become sarcastic with his students, and at home he resented doing "women's work." He became convinced that his wife was having an affair (which was false), and he had fantasies about running away. He felt that he had devoted himself to his wife, and now she was ignoring him. Rather than appreciating his efforts, she expected still more from him.

Lou had cycled through all three of the negative responses I outlined earlier. In the early stages of the marriage he was in the people-pleasing mode. Later, when they had children, he became domineering and abusive. When his wife threatened to leave, he again became a people-pleaser. Later, when the pressure eased, he became emotionally distant. This cyclical pattern is not unusual. Many men cycle through more than one pattern during the course of a marriage.

Obstacle 3: We have not learned to appreciate the differences in how men and women are taught to relate

One of the keys to change for a couple such as Lou and Sylvia is gaining an understanding of how their learned codes have determined their behavior in male-female relationships. These different codes have led to differences in language, beliefs, actions, and feelings.

These differences are summarized in the following table. I based the right side of the chart (about women) on research done at the Stone Center at Wellesley College on women's development. The material on the left side (about men) is based on my own observations.

Common Gender-Based Differences

Men	Women
Develop independence, self-reliance, autonomy	Develop and maintain relationships
Place importance on following personal dreams, destiny and self-fulfillment	Place importance on connectedness to others
Emphasize learning the rules (what's right or fair)	Emphasize learning empathy skills and relating
In a game, it's winning that counts	In a game, it's the personal relationships that counts
Emphasize competition	Emphasize cooperation
Conceal feelings (except anger)	Express feelings (except anger)
See danger in intimacy, feel threatened by own needs for attachment	See danger in impersonal achievement and competitive success
Fear loss of self through intimacy, experienced as invasion	Fear loss of self through intimacy, experienced as engulfment
Emphasize occupational growth	Emphasize family growth
See a problem and want to fix it	See a problem and want to talk about it

For boys, who are taught to achieve individual success through competition, knowing the rules of the game and playing to win is crucial. For girls, who are taught to develop relationships and connection, empathizing with others is crucial. If boys develop too much empathy, they can't effectively compete with each other because they will feel too sorry for their opponent. If girls become too competitive with other girls, they may not be able to maintain an empathetic disposition.

The three children of some friends of mine provide a perfect example of this. The two boys are highly competitive and successful in a variety of sports. These boys take great pleasure in defeating their friends in sporting activities. The girl is also gifted athletically. Yet, while she possessed great talent as a swimmer, she was reluctant to compete in swim meets until finally her parents were able to talk her into it. They were overjoyed when she won her event, but when they went to congratulate her, she was in tears. Their daughter was upset because she had defeated her best friend. She wanted never to swim competitively again because she feared losing her friends. Her parents were shocked. They were modern "gender-sensitive" parents who had not consciously raised their boys and girl differently. But the results were the same as in the old days.

Men and women also handle their emotional lives differently. Boys are taught to keep their emotions under control, with the possible exception of anger. Girls are taught to be sensitive to their own emotions as well as others', ironically with the possible exception of anger, which can jeopardize relationships.

Intimacy presents another important difference between males and females. Intimacy requires trust, which in turn necessitates relinquishing a degree of control. Thus men often find intimacy threatening to their independent identities. For women, being close to their mates and families is frequently perceived as essential to their identity. Men and women therefore often find their desires, for competition and intimacy, respectively, at odds.

The final dimension of gender differences is problem solving. Masculine conditioning requires us to be effective problem solvers. Many men pride themselves on their ability to fix anything and everything that is broken. Unfortunately, as we approach midlife we encounter many problems that are not easily put right. Our children have problems we can do nothing about, our health fails, people we love get sick and die.

Our propensity for trying to fix every problem can create its own problem with women. Women often want to be able to fix their problems on their own. They may want their mates to listen to their problems, but they may resent their husbands' immediate advice or their attempts to take care of the problem themselves.

Deborah Tannen, in *You Just Don't Understand*, provides several excellent examples of how these gender differences present obstacles for men and women in their relationships. Knowing that we speak a different language can help us be more understanding and patient in our marriages. But there are more ways to address the problem. In the next section I present other guidelines for change.

GUIDELINES FOR A NEW MODEL

I use the term *guidelines* rather than *rules* because reassessing our relationships with women has to be a very personal matter. We must each take a personal inventory of the ways we relate to women. These guidelines are intended to be a resource for that inventory.

I am sure each reader is already deeply involved in a reexamination of how he relates to women. In a sense my guidelines represent where I am in my own journey, but I have certainly not achieved perfection in following them. In fact, as with any type of major change in one's life, I struggle with these issues every day. Certain tensions always exist: Am I striking a proper balance between responding to women's needs and my own needs? Am I being too much of a nice guy or too much of a heel? How can I maintain the changes I desire without slipping back into old patterns?

1. Learn to be sensitive to your own feelings and needs. This was the message throughout the previous chapter, but it bears repeating. You cannot change how you relate to a woman until you change how you relate to yourself. You cannot care for another unless you care for yourself. If you attempt to change by accommodating to what women want without taking into account what you feel or want, your efforts will be doomed to failure.

Most men and women have the same basic needs in a relationship: to love and be loved. Any changes you make in a relationship need to begin with appreciation and acceptance of this point. You must be willing to give love if you expect to receive it. You must see your need to be loved as a strength, not as a weakness.

2. Recognize the three tenets of a successful relationship: intimacy, passion, and commitment. Intimacy means being willing to share yourself — your fears as well as your hopes and dreams. It also means being fascinated with your mate's inner life, even if her beliefs and secrets differ from yours.

Passion can be sexual, but it doesn't always have to be. Passion can also be an attitude: a sense of lovingness displayed toward your mate for who she is. It is a myth that passion fades in a relationship. When passion for your mate (or her passion for you) begins to diminish, it is time to take action. To do so requires commitment to the relationship.

Commitment means making the relationship your number one priority. Too many of us, consumed by work, let the marriage slip to second or even third or fourth priority in our lives. It is a myth to think that you fall in love, get married, and are happy ever after. If you intend to stay in your relationship, you have to be willing to persevere.

3. *Share your background and needs with your mate.* "Grant that we may not so much seek to be understood as to understand," says the St. Francis prayer . A healthy relationship depends on a balance of the two, an atmosphere of mutual understanding. A man's reticence can stifle a relationship because it leaves a woman puzzled about what makes him tick. It is particularly important to share those times when you feel diminished as man, whether from something that happened at work or at home. Most women do not understand that manhood is a constant test, that as men we feel shame if we have not measured up in some way. To keep these feelings to yourself means that all you present at home is your grumpy disposition with no explanation. To share them is to take a risk, but one that is necessary if you are to grow in your relationships.

It is also important to learn to understand and appreciate a woman's background and needs. Your mate's experience is vastly different from yours. As a female, she has been raised with a different set of values, different stories, different ways of looking at the world. To be committed to her means actively seeking to understand her story. Too many of us are more intent on changing her worldview than understanding it. You cannot change her lenses any more than she can change yours. This necessitates listening intently, without interruption, with your full attention. Even when you are not fascinated or when you do not agree with her, your active attention is important to her. Active listening means asking questions, really trying to understand, not just nodding yes while you read the paper or watch television.

4. Move from a competitive toward a cooperative relationship. Sometimes men are surprised at this suggestion because they do not consider themselves competitive in their relationships with their wives. Competitive at work? Yes. Competitive at sports? Certainly. But never in marriage! My experience in marital counseling reveals that competition is definitely present in most marriages, manifested in the allocation of resources, especially time and money. Where are we spending Christmas? Who is the better parent? Whose work is more important? Who is more understanding? Ad nauseam. This can be very destructive. As the competition increases, so does the bitterness and resentment.

To move to a cooperative, win-win orientation is difficult but crucial. Those in my men's groups who have managed to find happiness in their relationships identify this as the single most important step. Rather than viewing disagreements as power struggles, they view them as opportunities for discovery and understanding. Rather than thinking about "what is good for me," they think about "what is good for us." Rather than looking for ways to dominate a situation, they find ways to solve a problem through a compromise, where no one feels like a loser.

5. *Make a commitment to work through conflict without losing emotional control or running away.* Conflict is inevitable in any relationship. If handled correctly, it can increase understanding and produce growth. If handled poorly, it can be devastating. I believe couples should not strive to banish conflict from their relationships, but should seek mature resolutions of their disagreements. Let me suggest some ways to handle conflict constructively.

- Try to clarify your position by using "I" statements rather than "you" statements. "I" statements ("I am upset," "I want") places the responsibility for your beliefs, feelings, and behavior on you, not your spouse. "You" statements ("You made me mad," "You never give me any credit" etc.) blame the other party.

- Try to listen to the other person's point of view without getting emotionally reactive. Most important, let your mate finish her statements, even if you do not agree.

- Do not try to coerce your mate by raising your voice, inducing guilt, or issuing threats. Simply state how you see the situation and how you would like it resolved.

- If you or your mate feels like either of you is beginning to lose control, he or she is allowed to ask for a time out. Use this time to cool down. It is important to return, however. Just leaving the disagreement hanging is like leaving a smoldering fire. Keep trying to talk it through until you have reached some level of resolution.

6. Learn to apologize.   This tends to be very difficult for most men. Perhaps it is because men perceive any apology as an admission of error, which diminishes them as men. Apologize clearly and specifically, either in person or in writing, without any mention of the other's mistakes. Don't apologize expecting to receive an apology in return. This means no "I apologize, but you . . ." statements. Granted, apologizing is difficult to continue if you are always the only one doing it. But you may have to take the lead several times before you receive an apology in return. It's also important to try to change your behavior once the apology has been made rather than using the apology to absolve yourself of responsibility.

7. Accept the responsibility for healing your own pain. Do not expect your mate to heal your pain for you. I have pointed out in this book how many of us carry some wound (emotional or physical) from our childhood. When we get involved in a relationship with a woman, we often expect her to somehow heal this wound. We are essentially asking our mate to be the ideal mother who will take us in her arms and make the pain go away. But a healthy woman does not want to be our mother. She does not want to take on our pain. It is enough to have to deal with her own. Though it is appropriate and even necessary to share your feelings of vulnerability or pain with your mate, it is inappropriate to expect her to fix it.

Just as you are struggling to accept your own emotions, learn to accept those of your spouse. This is especially difficult when it comes to women's anger or pain. As men we've learned that we are supposed to fix things. When we see an angry or hurt woman, we assume it's our fault and somehow we're supposed to accept the responsibility to fix it. But often, we cannot do anything about it. We need to accept the woman's right to be angry and give up the notion that we can fix it by talking her out of it or by accommodating her wishes.

To heal your pain it is necessary to understand yourself in relation to your family of origin and to heal any strained relationships with them. As I have stated earlier, if a man does not deal with unfinished business in his family of origin, the spillover can destroy his own marriage. You must go home again, even if only to seek better understanding of yourself. Likewise it is crucial that you understand your mate in relationship to her family of origin. How you blend these two systems together is what marriage is all about. How to begin work with your own family of origin is the topic of chapter 7.

8. *Honestly assess the degree of responsibility you accept for doing household chores and caring for the children.* This is a tricky step. The husband's shirking of housework and child care is one of the main complaints women have about men. Many working women feel like they work two shifts — one at the office and a second one when they come home. They think their husbands do not do as much work as they do at home.

I believe it is especially crucial for a man to do some of the child care on a regular basis. This is not to placate the wife but to strengthen the bond between father and child.

An ideal situation, if it can be arranged, is for the father to take regular shifts of being in charge of the house and the children without his wife at home. This gives him a sense of understanding and mastery that he cannot achieve if his wife is home, when he might become resentful of her "orders."

Do not fall into the trap of being a provider as the only means of showing your love. Many men, especially workaholics, come to believe that by providing lavishly they are making their family happy. Time and time again, I hear women (and children) say that what they really want is for their husbands to spend more time with them. Giving of yourself is what matters most.

9. Find means of social and emotional support other than your wife. Earlier I described men's tendency to depend on one woman to fulfill numerous roles in their lives: lover, friend, social director, emotional support, and so forth. Placing so many expectations on one person can have dire consequences. It puts too much strain on the relationship. Seek support outside the marriage. (I am not talking here about developing a close relationship with another woman, which inevitably leads to jealousy.)

Male friendships are usually a low priority for us, coming in somewhere behind job, wife, kids, private time, and hobbies. Most men do not have another man to confide in. Yet friends can be a valuable resource.

Under the right circumstances, parents and siblings can also be marvelous sources of emotional and social support. Unfortunately in our mobile society men often move away from family and do not keep close connections. To reestablish these relationships requires devoting energy to them, through writing, phoning, and visiting.

10. Show your caring and nurturing side.   Even though we may feel uncomfortable with this side of ourselves, we have to learn to develop and express it. All human beings need and crave caring. Women, who generally have been brought up to do the care giving, need to receive it back, especially from their husbands. They in fact can teach us how to be caregivers. By observing them, we may learn how to do it ourselves. We can also learn from men who found ways to show they care.

One simple way to begin is to ask your wife regularly how she is doing, not in a cursory way but sincerely, with eye contact and undivided attention. Ask about her day and listen carefully to her answers. Asking further questions is a way of showing you care.

One other aspect of reassessing our relationships with women has to do with our sexual needs. I've devoted the entire next chapter to this important topic.

Setting Your Own Goals

Now that you have reviewed these guidelines, it is time once again to set goals for yourself. Review the steps and select a few that you would especially like to focus on. Write your goals on an index card or in your journal. Set a date to achieve them. Write down your plan for achieving them (how and why). Monitor your progress, and share your goals with someone who cares about you. Your mate might be a good person with whom to start, or perhaps you and a male friend can support each other in the process.

6 SEX: STILL CONFUSED AFTER ALL THESE YEARS

Men raised after World War II grew up in a society preoccupied with sex. Yet despite the media's obsession with sex, most men remain confused about their own sexuality and tend not to talk honestly with other men about it.

The following conversation, from my men's group, illustrates some of the confusing themes on men's minds.

During the round table discussion Rick, another member of the group, wanted to return to the topic of sex, which we had started a week earlier. "When I decided to marry for the third time, I realized I was taking a risk," he said. "Somehow marriage seems to kill sex. I could have sex every day, but it's not just the sex. I need love and affection. When we first started going together, the sex was great and frequent; but sure enough, since the wedding it's not the same. Only once or twice a week. I know I shouldn't feel so needy, but when she doesn't want to have sex, I feel there's something wrong with me."

Scott responded: "Rick, that's what you've got to get over. Just because she doesn't want to have sex, it doesn't mean there's something wrong with you. I've had to learn this lesson in my marriage. It ain't me. It's her issue. For a woman sex means something different. You can't take it so personally."

Arnie, too, wanted to help Rick. "It's the same with me and my wife. I say I want intimacy, affection, not just sex. The trouble is, she knows if she hugs me a lot or kisses me, I'll start to get turned on and get an erection. Then she assumes I want to have intercourse, even though I told her that's not what I want at all. But she feels guilty if she doesn't give me sex. So she just avoids the whole thing unless it's one of those nights when she does want to have sex."

Eric, a thirty-two-year-old stockbroker who had recently joined the group, overcame his awkwardness to contribute to the conversation. One year earlier his wife had remembered being sexually abused as a child. As the memories became more intense, she had difficulty engaging in sexual activity. Although Eric was extremely supportive of her, he had become increasingly frustrated about their lack of sexual intimacy. "I know not to take it personally," he told Rick, "but I know how you feel. As a kid I didn't get much affection, especially from my mother. Now when I don't get affection, I feel unwanted, unworthy. And given how difficult her situation is, I also feel ashamed for putting any pressure on her to have sex."

Derrick was even more uncomfortable with the conversation. His situation was the reverse of the others'. His wife wanted to have sex more often than he did, and over the past five years he had almost completely lost interest in sex, though he didn't come right out and say it to the group. Derrick was afraid something was terribly wrong with him, and, like Eric, he felt ashamed about himself sexually.

Frank, a thirty-eight-year old music producer, also felt some shame but for a different reason. He had lost interest in sex with his girlfriend, but he had resolved the problem by finding another lover. He had been up front with his girlfriend about the affair. In fact when they moved in together, Frank told her he did not believe in monogamy. Nevertheless he feared that the group would not accept his ideas about an open relationship. "I wonder why I lost interest in her," he said. "Maybe the physical part was too intimate, too close. I don't know. I knew I loved her, but I started to feel fenced in. It was too domestic, too intense. I think the turning point came when she wanted to get married. I just wasn't ready for that."

We are both fascinated and confused by sex. A recent Roper/Kinsey Institute poll confirmed that men lack basic information about sex. Among American males taking the test, 55 percent answered less than half of the eighteen multiple-choice questions correctly. Only 10 percent of the respondents correctly answered 80 percent or more of the items on fundamental sexual information. (I encourage you to read *The Kinsey Institute New Report on Sex* by June Reinisch and Ruth Beasley, which provides much more depth on this topic than I can. It is an excellent resource book on a sensitive and often mishandled subject.)

The media provides daily evidence of our proccupation with sexual matters and their complexities. In the two-month period of October to December 1991, for instance, a litany of stories relating to sexual behavior appeared in the papers and on television.

- Magic Johnson told a stunned nation that he had tested HIV-positive, having contracted the virus through extensive heterosexual activity. A national debate ensued on whether safe sex or abstinence was the solution to the problem, and another broke out on whether Johnson was a hero for speaking out or a villain for his sexual behavior.

- The entire nation was mesmerized by Anita Hill's claim that Supreme Court nominee Clarence Thomas had sexually harassed her ten years earlier. Americans were sharply divided over whom to believe. Hill's supporters felt strongly that the senators "just do not get it." Many men were left wondering exactly what it is they do not get.

- Roseanne Barr, LaToya Jackson (Michael's sister), and Marilyn Van Derber, a former Miss America, told the public they were sexually abused by their fathers or stepfathers. American men were shocked by the subsequent flood of disclosures from women with similar memories.

- Millions watched the William Kennedy Smith rape trial on television. Mr. Smith was eventually acquitted of the charges, but the issues it raised are still being debated, including what constitutes rape, whether a woman "asks for it," whether it's ever too late to say no, and whether a woman ever gets a fair trial when she accuses a man of rape.

Like most Americans, I followed these stories with interest. After years of repressing frank discussions of sexual matters, the media were suddenly openly addressing anything and everything. I had to wonder if this marked a new era of sexuality, one in which we can at last discuss some of these crucial issues openly, honestly, and objectively.

Contrary to the public's expectations, many middle-aged men would find such openness a great relief. We have had difficulty our entire lives reconciling our basic sexual urges and feelings with the prohibitions and secrecy that society has imposed on the subject. As a baby boomer born in 1946, I grew up in an era when sex was still a taboo subject. I can recall three incidents that manifested my own bewilderment about sex.

During my junior high school orientation, a group of guys from the elementary school in the working-class part of town asked me and my middle-class friends how many girls we "had had." I had only a vague sense of what they were talking about but was too embarrassed to ask them (or my friends) for clarification. I naively assumed the new kids had already "had" many, which, in retrospect, seems doubtful at best.

During the course of the year I became curious about a girl who seemed to miss a lot of school. When she was there, she often looked tired and disheveled. One day in shop class I heard a group of boys discussing her absences. "She's a whore," my friend Chuck explained to me. Once again I had only a vague notion of what that meant, so I decided to look the word up in the library's biggest dictionary. Sure enough, *whore* was listed, as were many other words I was confused about, like *vagina, penis,* and *intercourse.* Every few minutes I would sneak a look at another "dirty" word, but I didn't stay there too long for fear of being discovered. Even with my new knowledge, I was confused about the girl. Was she really a whore? Even if she was, how did Chuck and the other guys know? What was wrong with me that I didn't know and had to ask?

By far my most embarrassing memory from that year came from the gym locker room. An older boy I believed had flunked several times told me to check out the size of his penis. I must have looked petrified at his request, which I did not act on. So he told me that unless I met him in the boys' bathroom at 2:15 that afternoon, he was going to beat me up. Needless to say, I was filled with terror the rest of the day. I did not even consider telling a teacher. How would a twelve-year-old boy broach such a subject? Besides, whether I went or not, I figured that either way I was in serious trouble. I knew enough to assume that what he wanted me to do in the bathroom would horrify me. But being beaten up was nothing to look forward to either.

As the minutes ticked on in seventh-hour Spanish, I was frozen in dread. I told no one of my plight. I didn't know whether to ask Mr. Garcia for a bathroom pass or just sit still. I chose to sit and plotted my strategy for escaping from school at three o'clock.

Nothing did happen after school that Friday. The guy was nowhere to be seen, and as far as I can remember, I never saw him again. I never discussed any of these incidents with anyone. I did not even confide in my father, who had explained "the facts of life" to me a year earlier.

But what did the incidents have to do with a sperm and egg? I surely wasn't going to ask my parents about them. Nor was I going to admit my ignorance and confusion to my friends. No, I was just going to pretend that I was cool and understood exactly what was going on.

As I have worked with men over the years, I have learned that such situations — and my confusion and response — were by no means unique. Like me, most boys adopted the cool, silent stance when faced with bewildering questions of sexuality. We all tried to look like Elvis or Jimmy Dean, the embodiments of that confident, savvy look. Yet in reality we were lost little boys. When I talk to men at midlife about sexual concerns, many admit to feeling more like that uncomprehending little boy than the street-smart lover on the silver screen.

Even though society is changing in its views about sex, the legacy of growing up in an era when it was still a taboo subject remains a powerful influence on us.

SOURCES OF OUR CONFUSION

Social Change

To understand sexuality we must first recognize that sex is not just a biological phenomenon but also a social one. Standards of appropriate sexuality vary tremendously depending on the culture, the era, the context in which it occurs, and the stage of an individual's life.

The era after World War II was still characterized by the cultural message of the Puritans: Sex is bad, but parenthood is good. However, the rebellion in the 1960s against this repressive horror, the creation of the birth-control pill, which made it possible to have sex without the high risk of pregnancy, and the women's liberation movement all combined to spawn a sexual revolution.

In a relatively brief period (approximately 1965 to 1970) sexual behavior changed radically. Men and women first experienced intercourse at steadily lower ages, unmarried couples began living together, and casual sex became the accepted norm in society.

But, contrary to popular opinion, the revolution was not complete. Although the old patterns of sexual behavior were rejected, no clear new model emerged to take its place. More important, our old beliefs did not keep pace with our new actions.

According to Sylvia Hacker, a noted expert on sex education, "In the climate of 'doing your own thing,' controls were virtually abandoned. However, even though behaviors changed rapidly, the old, deeply ingrained, erotophobic attitudes lingered. Sex was still accompanied by shame, guilt, and embarrassment" (Sylvia Hacker, "The Transition from the Old Norm to the New," *Sex Information and Education Council Report* 18, 5 [1990]: 3). This is still true to a large extent as we remain in an era of transition. The sexual revolution is now faced with a much bigger threat: AIDS. Even with the increase in information, protection, and restraint, it seems unlikely that we will go back to the repressed attitudes of the 1950s.

An important question is, Did the sexual revolution really liberate us? When men in my groups consider their sexual lives, few feel liberated. Even though society has become more open about sex, we still have a paucity of information about our bodies and our emotions in relation to our sexual lives. It may be that we are more active than previous generations, but most men still do not feel fully comfortable with their sexuality. For many, sex has remained a mysterious drive that brings not only intense pleasure but a surprising measure of shame and guilt.

Do I Measure Up?

The second source of our discomfort with sexuality is our obsession with keeping score, comparing ourselves with other men. This statistical fixation generally dwells on these items:

- How big is my penis? Is that big enough?
- How long can I hold my erection during inter-course?
- How many times in a row can I come?
- How fast and frequently can I bring my mate to orgasm? In how many ways?
- How many times a week do I have sex?
- How many women have I "had"?
- Do I have the qualities that attract women?

This focus on performance has snuffed our ability to enjoy sex. Rather than being an exquisitely pleasurable, shared expression of affection, it becomes a duty or com-petition, with performance criteria as cold and uncompro-mising as those of the corporation. How can we enjoy ourselves if we are blinded by judging how well we are performing or how we compare to others?

This obsession with comparison contributes to the three most common concerns men have about sex: their penis size, premature ejaculation, and frequency of intercourse.

Almost every male has, at one time or another, suf-fered from a fixation about the size of his penis. "I'll show you mine, if you show me yours" is a challenge familiar to every male who spent time on a playground. This score-keeping is heightened during puberty and when men begin their sexual explorations.

It is not surprising, therefore, that many men exag-gerate their anatomical dimensions and impress upon others the advantage that gives them in attracting and pleasing women.

What we ignore, however, in our concern over "normal" or "desirable" anatomy is the fact that it has little to do with a woman's biological sexual pleasure or her preferences. According to the Kinsey survey, the average-size penis is between five and seven inches and has little or no effect on men's appeal to women or to women's pleasure. The old saw "It's not the song but the singer" turns out to be true. Dwelling on size is not only a waste, it is irrelevant to sexual appeal and satisfaction.

In terms of males' sexual fears, premature ejaculation is a close second. Ironically it is almost always related to a man's fear that he will not be able to hold his erection long enough. When I asked men how long is long enough, their answers vary tremendously, from two minutes to two hours. When asked why they believe it needs to be so long, they inevitably claim that it's vital "to satisfy my partner" or because "that's what a man should do." Yet research has shown that a woman's sexual pleasure is not directly related to how long a man has intercourse before ejaculating.

First of all, one third to one half of all women rarely experience orgasm during intercourse. They need manual or oral stimulation of the clitoris to reach orgasm. So, no matter how long a man "lasts," it will probably not lead to orgasm.

Second, it may not be a question of duration but of quality, a definition that varies tremendously from woman to woman. A consistent belief among most women, however, is that men often focus on their stamina to the detriment of communication. Asking about her needs and desires, and communicating his, tend to be far more important in building sexual excitement than stamina.

Arnie had read many books about sexuality and knew intellectually that there was nothing wrong with him when he reached orgasm "too quickly" according to an arbitrary norm that he had established. His wife also reassured him that how long he remained erect did not matter to her. Yet each time Arnie had sex with her, he worried that he would reach orgasm too quickly. When he did come sooner than he would have liked, he felt guilty, inadequate, and upset with himself over his "poor performance." Even though Arnie could recognize that the time it took him to reach orgasm had more to do with the frequency of sex than with his adequacy as a man, he still could not shake his fear and sense of inadequacy.

Eric, one of the members of the group, advised Arnie to think negative thoughts to distance himself and prolong his "performance," like worrying about money or a problem at the office. But as soon as Eric heard himself say this, he began to laugh. He realized that he was advising Arnie to turn a joyous experience into another worry in order to prolong his pleasure.

The performance hang-up also prompts men to quantify and compare the frequency of their sexual experiences. Gil, a thirty-two-year-old fireman, was a classic case. He fretted that there was something terribly wrong with him because he didn't want to have sex more than once or twice a month, and he had heard from the guys in the firehouse that the national average was once or twice a week. Consequently he tried to stimulate his desire by watching pornographic movies on a regular basis. This sudden habit upset his wife, and also unnerved Gil, who felt he could not compete with the exaggerated action and atypical bodies on the screen. After a few months of this, he found his desire not increasing but waning.

It was during this period that Gil lost his erection midway through intercourse with his wife, which created even more self-doubt. He feared that he would lose his erection again, so he withdrew almost completely from sexual activity. Naturally his wife perceived this as rejection, which consequently made him feel even guiltier. By the time they sought out a marriage counselor, their sex life was completely dormant.

In therapy the couple learned that desiring sex once or twice a month is not abnormal nor a sign of a serious problem. It is merely the reflection of Gil's particular sexual drive or appetite. If his wife wanted sex more often, she could be satisfied by stimulation through noncoital ways. In fact, she acknowledged that she enjoyed this attention as much as intercourse. She was concerned not about the frequency of intercourse but about Gil's seemingly diminished interest in her. Armed with new information and improved communication, the couple once again began to enjoy a satisfying and healthy sex life on their own terms.

Sex and Shame

Because we were raised in an era of sexual repression, we may feel a vague sense of shame about sexual matters, though intellectually we know sex is normal and healthy. These are the most common guilt inducers:

Masturbation.   Most men grew up believing that masturbation was evil. Many myths were perpetuated about self-stimulation: that it was abnormal, sinful, and could cause pimples, hairy palms, sterility, and even insanity. Obviously these are all false.

Fantasizing. Most men (and women) in the baby-boom generation picked up another message from their parents— that there was little distinction, if any, between fantasy and activity. Imagining a sexual scenario was therefore almost as bad as acting it out. Consequently common fantasies about a variety of sexual acts with a variety of partners— including teachers, classmates, and strangers— engendered intense guilt in many young men. If these acts were deemed perverse (or illegal), then thoughts of them had the same effect on the male's conscience.

We know now that such fantasies are only a problem if they are translated into behavior, and then only a problem if that behavior is inappropriate or illegal. Fantasizing may also become a problem if a person requires it in order to achieve arousal and climax.

According to almost every study on the subject, virtually everyone— male or female— has engaged in masturbation and fantasizing, and most on a regular basis. The next two items, however, are less common experiences for the majority of people, although we're discovering that many more people have had these experiences than we originally thought.

Being a victim of sexual abuse. This shame is so deep-seated that many people totally repress their memories of the incident(s). Such repression was accurately depicted in the book (and movie) *Prince of Tides.* The main character, Tom, was able to describe the rape of his mother and sister by escaped convicts to his sister's psychiatrist. Yet he had repressed the fact that he, too, had been raped by the fugitives. Through his work in psychotherapy, Tom is finally able to recall his own rape and the attending emotions.

While in recent years the media has focused considerable attention on the sexual abuse of girls, relatively little
has been said about the sexual abuse of boys. Yet several
research studies indicate that approximately 16 percent of
men report having been sexually abused during their
youth (as compared to 27 percent of women). Researchers
believe that "boys may be victimized by sexual abuse
more than is generally believed, perhaps even as frequently as girls, but are much less likely to report it" (*New
York Times*, January 13, 1987).

This reluctance relates to the male mandate to act
strong and keep things to yourself. If a boy is abused, he
believes that it is his fault, that he must have done something to provoke the act. If the molester was male, the victim may suspect himself of homosexuality, fearing that he
promoted the abuse because somehow he was perceived as
welcoming the sexual attention of another man.

Having victimized someone sexually. The definition of
our sexual "shadow sides" varies greatly from man to
man. In one men's group, Ken bragged about his prowess
in seducing women, while Richard felt guilty for having
convinced a teenage girl to have sex with him. Likewise
Ben thought that taking a prostitute along on a hunting
trip was adventurous and manly, while Lance regarded the
same act as morally reprehensible.

The vast majority of men who engage in any facet of
this wide spectrum of sexual conduct feel guilt over it.
And unless they've committed an illegal act and been
arrested for it, they probably have never talked to anyone
about their past behavior.

Mark, a well-respected fifty-five-year-old small business owner, hardly fit the stereotype of the exhibitionist.

He was well respected in the community and the father of three grown children. Yet he was arrested for masturbating in a public mall and was so ashamed he told no one about it, including his wife. Mark's history was fairly typical of the sexual abuser:

1. He had a pattern of out-of-control sexual behavior, including masturbating in a phone booth while watching women walk by.

2. He had suffered severe consequences for his behavior but persisted despite the risks, having been arrested once for a similar act (though he was not prosecuted). His wife knew of his first arrest and threatened to leave him if it happened again.

3. He had made frequent attempts to break the pattern but refused to go for help until ordered by the court. He believed he could manage the behavior by himself.

4. Mark almost always got drunk before engaging in the destructive behavior.

5. Like other sexual abusers, he denied the severity and risk of the behavior.

6. Like the vast majority of sexual abusers, he himself had been sexually abused, in this case by another boy, who forced him to perform fellatio when he was ten.

After his second arrest, Mark seriously considered suicide, but an abiding faith in God, coupled with the help of Alcoholics Anonymous, his wife, and a therapist, enabled

Mark to successfully recover from this pattern. Like a recovering alcoholic, Mark still — three years into his treatment — acknowledges his potential to revert to his old behavior.

(If after reading this section, you believe you may be a sexual addict, I would strongly suggest you read *Don't Call It Love* by Patrick Carnes, *Victims No Longer* by Mike Lew, attend a Sexual Addicts Anonymous group and see a therapist who specializes in sexual abuse. It is usually a problem that cannot be solved without outside help.)

Homophobia

Homophobia, according to the Kinsey Institute, has five dimensions: hatred of gays, fear of gays, fear that homosexuality is contagious, fear that people will think you are gay, and repression of one's own homosexual feelings.

In the United States homophobia is so strong that it warps many of our beliefs and actions. For many straight men, the thought of being homosexual is quite abhorrent. Our culture depicts homosexuals as deviant, inferior, and "not really men." Even before they understand sexuality, boys put other boys down by calling them "fags" or "queers." At a young age boys who somehow fail to adhere to strict standards of male behavior are derided as "sissies" and "mama's boy's." At that age it has nothing to do with sexual behavior, but in adolescence sexual feelings are shaped by the admonitions of the male code of sexual behavior. The strongest of these states that "real men" are attracted only to women. Many men interpret the slightest sign of attraction to another male as proof of their own or another man's homosexual tendencies.

Yet Alfred Kinsey's research into sexual preference indi-

cates that such a black-and-white model of sexual preference is inaccurate. Men and women are not strictly heterosexual or homosexual; rather we fall into a continuum
of sexual preference ranging from totally heterosexual to
totally homosexual. Most fall somewhere between the two
extremes.

Kinsey revealed that 37 percent of the men he interviewed reported having had "some overt homosexual
experience to the point of orgasm between adolescence
and old age." This finding shattered the belief that homosexuality was an extremely unusual pattern of behavior.

Kinsey's research led him to formulate a seven-point
scale that ranges from zero, indicating exclusive heterosexual behaviors and interests, to six, indicating exclusive
homosexual behaviors and interests (see fig. 2). Based on

Figure 2. Kinsey's Homosexual Rating Scale

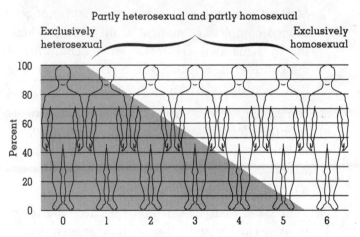

Source: Adapted from Alfred C. Kinsey et al., Sexual Behaviour in the
Human Male *(Philadelphia: Saunders, 1948), p. 638. Reproduced by
permission of the Kinsey Institute for Research in Sex, Gender, and
Reproduction, Inc.*

Kinsey's model, we can comfortably estimate that over one third of all males will have some homosexual experience in their lives. If one third have acted on this desire, it is plausible to speculate that many more males will have an occasional sexual fantasy about other men but choose not to act on this fantasy.

Yet due to the extreme homophobia in our society, powerful feelings of guilt or shame accompany any sexual inclinations or actions toward other males. To counteract such feelings, males develop strong antipathy toward homosexuals and toward that part of ourselves which may have feelings for other men. This can have various effects on our behavior and on the lives of gay men.

1. Men are reluctant to hug or touch other men because it might be interpreted as a sign of homosexuality.

2. Men are reluctant to dress in a way that is not considered completely "manly." Until recently, dressing in a manner counter to strict definitions of masculine attire was thought to be an indication of homosexual tendencies.

3. Some men feel they have to have control sexually over their female partners, because letting a women initiate actions could be construed as a sign of weakness. This in turn is associated with homosexuality in the minds of many men.

4. Men avoid male friendships. Men fear that emotionally close relationships with other men may be viewed as, or develop into, a homosexual relationship. Further, if a man finds another man physically attractive, he might fear he is a closet homosexual.

5. Our prejudice sometimes endangers homosexuals. Homosexuals have been beaten and even murdered simply because of their sexual preference. But they also face impediments to job advancement and social acceptance once they have come out.

6. Hostility toward homosexuals understandably affects their mental well-being. Many are afraid to admit their sexual preference because they know how they will be treated by other males and by their own families. Many try to conceal their sexual preference for years either by abstaining from relationships or by entering into heterosexual relationships.

One such person who concealed his sexual preference was a high school classmate of mine, Carl, who told me and many of our peers of his homosexuality at our twentieth reunion in 1984. I had respected Carl since I first met him in junior high, but I had not seen him since we graduated from the same college in 1968. Though I was shocked by his declaration years later, I also admired his courage for being so honest.

Nonetheless I never quite got around to looking Carl up or writing him after that reunion. Looking back on it, I was probably unsure how to handle his openness about his sexual preference. I was jolted out of my uncertainty when I visited Ken, a mutual friend, in New York City in 1990. Ken had done a much better job communicating with Carl than I had, and I was stunned to learn that Carl had contracted AIDS.

As soon as I returned home I wrote Carl a letter. Two weeks later his sister called to inform me that Carl had died two days before my letter arrived.

My grief was diminished by the trust Carl's sister placed in me. Knowing I was a writer, she trusted me with Carl's extensive journals and letters, hoping that I could communicate Carl's insights on homosexuality and AIDS.

The materials I read, stretching back to Carl's teens, provided much more. In his early journals he described his struggles to come to terms with his homosexuality, which he had been aware of since boyhood. To conceal his sexual preference, he went so far as to marry, though he had no children. This repression brought on several predictable side effects, including alcoholism and depression. In midlife he finally accepted his homosexuality, divorced, started attending Alcoholics Anonymous, and began to rediscover happiness.

He turned to writing and pursued his interests in gardening and Latin-American culture. Even when he learned in 1987 that he had AIDS, he lived his life with enthusiasm and dignity. The following excerpt is from a letter to his only nephew, then ten years old, and is a clear and beautiful manifestation of his spirit:

August 25, 1987

Dear Michael,

... Your mom and Grandma think you are too young to understand something I must tell you. They think that little boys aren't ready to face bad or embarrassing news. I disagree! I know you are a fine young man with all the courage and strength that the rest of us have. You are grown up and old enough to understand. And you are stubborn enough to form your own opinions whether we like it or not! You are also smart enough to choose your opinions with good sense.

So here comes my deep dark secret. I am gay and I have AIDS. Frank, the man you met at my house and the man who spent Christmas at your house two years ago, is also gay and he is in the hospital with a very serious case of AIDS. Frank and I were companions for many years and we loved each other, just the way your Mom and Dad love each other. Both Frank and I have an illness, just plain illness that you go to the doctor for. Unfortunately, AIDS is an illness that can kill you. Unless the doctors find some new medicine, we will probably die in a few years....

... Some day you will be the only person left to carry on the traditions of the family. We all trust you to do an even better job of it than we have been able to do.

Please don't start to worry about me yet. I only have the very early stages of AIDS. I feel healthy and happy. I'm not contagious, and I have a lot of time left to love, and visit, and be proud of my nephew.

> With a big hug and
> a punch in the shoulder,
>
> Your loving Uncle Carl

Sexual Self-Evaluation

Before proceeding to the next section, take time to reflect on how each of these factors has affected your sexual self. Use the table included here as a guide to make some notes on your own sexual history.

Source of Confusion	How Your Sexual Self Relates to the Source
Sex was a taboo subject.	Reflect on your early learning about sexuality.
Sexual norms have changed.	Reflect on your sexual history. As times changed, how did you change?
Do I measure up?	How were you influenced by the pressure to meet certain sexual standards?

Homophobia.	How has homophobia influenced your view of yourself and other males? How do you feel about homosexuals?
Being a victim or perpetrator of sexual abuse.	Were you sexually abused in any manner? Have you sexually abused someone else?
Feeling shame and guilt about sexuality.	To what extent has shame colored your views of yourself sexually? Do you still feel ashamed of your sexual self?
The role of women has changed.	How have changes in women's views of themselves sexually changed your views of your sexual self?

Disregarding what you "should" or "should not" want, consider what you truly have liked and disliked about the sexual experiences in your life. Listing them is often helpful.

STEPS TOWARD A MORE FULFILLING SEXUAL SELF

In this section I present some guidelines that may help you improve your sexual happiness — as distinct from "performance," which has been our greatest obstacle in reaching sexual satisfaction. These guidelines are intended to help you better understand your sexual self, to clarify what you want and need sexually, and to help you overcome problems from your sexual past.

Step 1. Identify and challenge your prevailing myths about sexuality.   In reviewing the literature about sexuality, I have identified some of the most common sexual myths that many men (and women) still believe. The first step toward sexual health is to review the list and identify those you still hold as true.

Myth 1: Sex is performance.   Many men believe that to be a good lover they must be able to restrain themselves sufficiently to satisfy their partners. A healthier alternative is to believe that sex is pleasure. Belief in the old myth can transform sex into work.

Myth 2: The man is responsible for the woman's pleasure. This is related to the first myth: if a man can hold off his orgasm long enough, his partner will reach an orgasm. Actually, less than 50 percent of women are orgasmic during intercourse when the only form of stimulation is penile thrusting; many women prefer being stimulated manually or orally (or stimulating themselves); not all women want orgasms every time they have sex; and the woman often prefers to be an active partner in sex rather than leaving it up to the male to be the active sexual partner.

Myth 3: Sex means intercourse only, and preferably without a condom.   In an era when AIDS deaths are multiplying, intercourse without a condom is potentially lethal. Sexual satisfaction can be derived from many means other than intercourse, and using the wide array of condoms now available can greatly increase stimulation for both partners. Putting the condom on can be an enjoyable part of foreplay.

Myth 4: Men have a higher sex drive than women; men who don't are abnormal. To a large extent sex drive in both men and women is related to testosterone levels. Research shows that two thirds of men and one third of women have high levels of testosterone. The determinant of testosterone levels is strictly biological, nothing else. "Normal" is whatever is comfortable for you and your partner.

Myth 5: A man should be ready for sex whenever and wherever, no matter what his mood. Men have somehow learned that it is not manly to decline sexual opportunities. We hold to the silly notion that even if we are tired, in a bad mood, or worried, we should be ready to perform the moment our mates indicate their desire. This should not be expected of us or of women.

Myth 6: Great lovers are born, not made. Simply being born male is supposed to bestow on us tremendous skill as lovers. The truth is that loving is a learned pattern, born out of familiarity with ourselves and our partners. With increased knowledge, experience, and self-acceptance any man can become a satisfying lover.

Myth 7: Penis size is directly related to a woman's sexual pleasure. According to research, this is simply not true. Satisfying sex is not a function of penis size but depends on how well a man uses his penis and his other sexual organs (hands, mouth, and especially his mind). Most women will tell you the mind is the most powerful aphrodisiac available.

Myth 8: Masturbation is a sign of weakness or inadequacy. In fact, it is not physically or emotionally harmful nor a sign of weakness in males or females. Masturbation is simply a healthy sexual outlet, no more, no less.

Myth 9: Sex with a new partner is better than with a longtime companion. Having built strong trust and communication, longtime companions know each other so well that their sex life is usually far more satisfying than sex with relative strangers. The newness and secrecy of a new relationship can be exciting, of course, but the pleasure diminishes as the novelty wears off.

Myth 10: Sex should be a man's primary source of release, without which his level of achievement will suffer. Sex is obviously a wonderful release, but if a man depends on it as his only emotional outlet, he is headed for trouble. As we learned in chapter 4, it is crucial for men to develop their emotional selves and to learn to express emotions in a variety of ways. Furthermore, there is no evidence linking sexual intercourse to achievement. If a man feels sexual tension, he can relieve it through masturbation as well as he can through intercourse. A good run or a workout might suffice.

Myth 11: If your partner loves you, she will know what you need sexually without asking. The reality is that love and knowledge of sexual needs are not related. Communication between partners is the necessary ingredient for understanding each other's sexual needs.

After reviewing these myths, note which ones apply to you, and consider how they might impede your sexual functioning. You can begin to challenge these myths today.

Step 2. Learn to recognize and accept your sexual needs. The following questions can help you in this process.

- Consider the ways you feel sexually vulnerable. What do you fear or dislike about your sexual self?

- Are you clear about the distinction between your needs for intimacy and your sexual needs? Many people confuse the two. Intimacy means feeling close and secure with another person, and may or may not involve sexual contact. Can you feel intimate with your partner without directing the experience toward sex?

- Men also frequently confuse sexual response with acceptance by their partner. They see sex as the ultimate form of acceptance, and if their partner does not want to have sex they feel rejected. Acceptance can be expressed in many ways. Can you recognize alternative expressions of acceptance?

- Are you clear about the distinction between sexual fantasies and behavior? A person's thoughts, feelings, and fantasies are private matters and are rarely problems unless they are acted upon. Even then they are not harmful unless one impose one's will on a partner without consent.

- Do you have core emotional issues that get played out in your sexual relations? Examples include fear of abandonment; the need to control circumstances and people; a compulsive need for order or cleanliness; fear of women; and fear of emotional release. It is important to identify such issues and develop a plan for dealing with them.

- Do you use sex to manipulate others? People sometimes use sex (or the withholding of sex) to dominate, control, or humiliate their mates — all common themes in movies. Sex is also used to sell us products. Using sex as a vehicle for other desires can be destructive, affecting a relationship's sexual and emotional facets.

- What obstacles must you overcome to communicate nonsexual feelings to your partner? Communication strategies will be addressed in step 7.

Step 3. Identify and heal your sexual wounds. Having grown up in a confused sexual era, we inevitably experienced sexual wounds and humiliations somewhere in our development. Likewise it is not unusual for males to have harmed others out of ignorance. For our sexual health we must recognize and accept these events from the past. Only in this way can we prevent their recurrence in the future and begin the process of healing.

Examine whether you have ever been sexually abused, which includes any violation of your sexual boundaries against your will. This may have been by a family member, an authority figure (such as a teacher, health-care provider, scout leader, or clergyman), or a peer.

According to Patrick Carnes (*Don't Call It Love: Recovery from Sexual Addiction* [New York: Bantam Books, 1991]), the most common types of sexual abuse experienced by males who are treated for sexual addiction are these: (contact forms) inappropriate holding and kissing, sexual fondling, masturbation, oral sex, forced sexual activities; (noncontact forms) flirtations and suggestive language, propositions, household voyeurism and exhibitionism, sexualizing language, and preoccupation with sexual development.

If you have been the victim of sexual abuse or suspect you may have been, you need to start the healing process. Possible steps include reading more about the topic. Michael Lew's *Victims No Longer* and Ellen Bass and Laura Davis's *The Courage to Heal* have helped hundreds of thousands of people. Talking to someone about your experience also helps tremendously. Your mate, a friend, a therapist, or a Twelve-Step support group are probably your best outlets.

It is also possible that, according to these criteria, you have sexually abused someone else. Have you used force or coercion to get someone to have sex with you? This naturally raises the question of where to draw the line between undue coercion and benign seduction. Do you and your partner currently have some agreement on acceptable standards?

If you have victimized others, you also need to start the process of healing. First you need to make a commitment to yourself to no longer be abusive to others. Sharing your secret with someone you trust is important.

If the victim is someone you still know, a heartfelt apology, as painful as it might be, will do much to heal both of you. (If you no longer have contact with the person, it is a more complicated issue. Writing a letter of apology is crucial; the question is whether or not to send the letter. This is a matter best discussed in therapy.) If your problem is ongoing you need to get outside help immediately through therapy, a recovery program, or a Twelve-Step group.

Step 4. *Recognize and challenge your feelings and beliefs about homosexuality.*   When I first broach this topic in my men's groups, most of the participants consider it irrelevant. They do not see at first that their fears about homosexuality take their toll on their relationships with other heterosexual men and on their relationships with women, especially wives or girlfriends.

Consider to what degree you maintain myths about homosexual men, discussed earlier. The most common

myths include the notion that sexual orientation is heterosexual or homosexual, with no middle ground; that
gay males suffer from a confused masculine identity; that
they hate or fear women; that they have an insufficient
amount of testosterone; or that they are generally
unhappy and are likely to foist their sexual orientation on
those around them, particularly the young.

If you react negatively to homosexuals, do you understand why? Is it based on what you learned in your youth,
stereotypes, or a lack of familiarity with them? Have you
ever really known a gay man?

Do you harbor fears that you may be homosexual or
bisexual? Do these fears influence your life in some
uncomfortable ways?

Step 5. Learn more about sex.   Though we grew up in
an era of confusion and ignorance about sex, the good
news is that we can do something about it. There are
many valuable resource books on sex. These go a long way
toward dispelling myths, providing ideas on how to get
out of uncomfortable sexual patterns, and avoiding health
problems. They can help you to become a better lover and
to better understand your sexual self and sexual partners.
(See Suggested Reading at the end of this book.)

*Step 6. Take responsibility for the care of your sexual
self.*   This maturity starts with birth control. Lest we forget, sex can lead to reproduction. Whatever a man's age,
he is capable of producing children. Research shows that
the vasectomy is the safest and surest form of birth control. It does not diminish sexual performance or increase
health risks.

Learn about AIDS and other sexually transmitted diseases. You need to know how they are transmitted so that you can take all due precautions. I am amazed at how many of my clients still refuse to use condoms when having sex with a new partner. They labor under the potentially deadly assumption that if a woman seems responsible, she will not be a carrier of a sexually transmitted disease. Get tested.

Taking care of your other health needs is also vital. Being healthy and feeling good about yourself physically are keys to a satisfying sex life. Finally, accept masturbation as a useful way to take care of your sexual needs if a partner is not available.

Step 7. Improve communication and cooperation in your relationship(s). The steps of this process focus on self-exploration and communication and cooperation with a partner.

First, communicate with each other honestly about your sexual needs, preferences, desires, and concerns. These conversations should go on both in and out of bed. It can help to bring the topic up first away from the bedroom, when neither partner is in a sexual mood. This frees you of the hidden agenda of using the talk as a way to lead to sex.

Once the dialogue has begun away from the bedroom, it should be continued the next time you are in bed to give each other specific feedback about what feels good and what doesn't. We carry around many assumptions about what constitutes pleasure for our mates, but often these are not correct or only sporadically so. A mutually satisfying sex life develops through feedback between partners. Your mate is not clairvoyant. It is not unmanly to ask.

You will also need to understand and respect each other's sexual boundaries. This doesn't mean you have to ask if each step in the sexual process is acceptable, but it does mean that you cannot coerce your partner into crossing the boundary if she objects. If there is a sexual activity about which you disagree, discuss it away from the bed so you will not be under the influence of sexual desire.

Another step toward cooperation is to work together to remove the score card from your sex life. Instead of focusing on numbers — how many, how often, and so forth — focus on quality — how pleasurable, how thoughtful, how spiritual. Moving toward a view of sex as creative, playful, and meaningful can be a renewing and remarkably erotic experience.

Cooperation also entails accepting the differences you may have in your level of sexual desire. It is entirely possible to have a satisfying sex life despite these differences as long as both persons have some sexual desire. But you must acknowledge and understand the differences and together think through ways to handle your differences. Again, masturbation is an acceptable outlet for either partner. If one partner seems to have no sexual desire, however, the couple should seek outside help.

Communicating about sexual needs means determining what priority we'll give to sex. In today's busy world, sex cannot be expected to happen spontaneously. Dual careers, children, and housework create busy schedules that interfere with sex. Decide together how important sex is for you, make accommodations accordingly, and then structure your environment to maximize the opportunities.

- Make your bedroom a lovely place.

- Remove the TV from the bedroom.

- Set aside time when you can be alone without the children.

- Go away on romantic retreats.

- Make dates.

- Coordinate your sleep cycles.

- Learn to signal to each other your interest in being sexual.

- Think about what turns your partner on (in the new sexuality your doing the dishes can be a bigger turn on than wearing cologne).

Many people mistakenly believe they can improve their sex lives by finding another partner. Although this may be true in the short run, they take a great risk by experimenting outside of the committed relationship before resolving the problems in a relationship. If you are considering an affair, try first to work on your current relationship.

Nothing complicates marital problems like an affair. The secrecy of the affair destroys trust between the couple. Furthermore, it is difficult to compare sex with an extra-marital partner to sex with a longtime companion. Forbidden fruit has an undeniable appeal — the fact that it is "wrong" lends it much of its excitement. The new, secret sex will feel exhilarating compared to sex in a troubled relationship, but this does not mean sex with the new partner will remain great. Once the thrill vanishes, rather than having one partner to resolve problems with, you now have two.

I am not trying to be prudish here, merely rational. I recognize that the temptation to have an affair is great for all those who have been in a long-term relationship. The temptation is as inevitable as early adolescent love. Yet to act on it is to take a tremendous risk. My strong recommendation is that you first be honest with your mate regarding your feelings about your marriage and your temptations. Seek counseling. If you can't work out your marital difficulties, decide whether or not you want to stay in the relationship, independent of the affair. If you conclude that things have run their course, move out, grieve, live for a while on your own. This will help ensure you are not getting involved with someone else simply for the appeal of a mischievous act, with only short-term payoffs.

Step 8. Teach your children well. Make a commitment to teach your children about healthy sexuality. Obviously you first need to educate yourself so you are comfortable and knowledgeable talking about sex. If they don't feel comfortable talking about sex, which is quite common, you might leave sex education books around where they can pick them up. When they are curious, they will talk to you about them, which they will also do after some movies and TV shows. Assure them that they can tell or ask you absolutely anything, and you will not shame or embarrass them. Talk to other parents (especially fathers) for good ideas.

The most effective means of education, of course, is to set a good example. You can do this by being open and honest with yourself about your own sexual experience, beliefs, and desires. Knowledge of sexual matters and yourself is power; with it you can lead a healthy, satisfying sex life and help your partner and children do the same.

7 OUR PARENTS, OURSELVES, OUR CHILDREN: TOWARD UNDERSTANDING AND HEALING

This chapter's purpose is twofold: first, to help the reader better understand his parents and begin healing his relationship with them; and second, to help the reader be a better father to his children.

To become a better parent, a man needs to come to terms with his own parents. To misunderstand his parents, to avoid talking seriously with them, or to cling to his bitterness and resentment toward them is to risk repeating the same harmful patterns with his own children.

Each generation needs to go through the process of healing its relationship with the previous generation. Why? Because the act of parenting is so challenging, so demanding, so fraught with danger that no matter how hard we try to be good parents, we will inevitably cause some pain for our offspring.

Sy SaFransky writes eloquently about this reality. "We were all wounded in some way by our parents; not because they were evil, or wished us harm, but because they too were wounded, like their parents before them. . . . Thus the pain echoes sorrowfully, from generation to generation — while we, yearning desperately for our own measure of happiness, discover no amount of food will fill our emptiness, no lover will banish the memory of a mother's absence or a father's scorn."

Sam's case illustrates this. A human resource director in his late thirties, Sam came to see me about troubles in his marriage. After several sessions he decided he wanted to invite his father to a session to address the severe physical punishment he had inflicted on Sam when he was young. His seventy-four-year-old father agreed.

At first Sam's father, Ed, was hurt and confused. He was aware that his son had been avoiding him for several years, but he couldn't understand why. Like most fathers, Ed sincerely believed, perhaps rightly, that he had done the best job he could do to raise his son.

The old man listened respectfully as the son chronicled his memories of the severe beatings. When his son finished, he sat motionless for several minutes. I didn't know whether he was trying to keep from exploding or fighting back the tears — probably both.

Finally Ed began his response, "Sam, I've heard what you said, and I'm not going to sit here and deny any of it, nor am I going to try to make excuses. I'm sorry if I hurt you, but I would like you to understand that in my own way I was trying to do the best I could.

"You may not know this, but when you were born, I had no idea how to be a father. My father left when I was born, and I was raised by a series of stepfathers and my mother's boyfriends. Each seemed to hate and resent me more than the one before. They paid so little attention to me that I didn't mind the spankings because at least I was getting some attention from a man.

"When I married your mother and we started to have children, I vowed I would never leave her and would provide for all my children. And this is what I've done.

I didn't know shit about kids or love or discipline or anything. I probably worked too many hours. And yes, I know I was too rough on you. But that was nothing compared to how I was treated. I didn't know how to talk to you to get you to mind, so I hit you. That's what I thought a good father was supposed to do.

"If I hurt you, and I apparently did, I'm sorry, but . . ."

With this he paused. I was praying he'd tell Sam he loved him, which he had never done before. But he didn't. He just slumped in his chair, staring at the rug. Apparently these words were not part of this man's vocabulary. Seeing the two men frozen in their chairs, avoiding eye contact, I wanted to urge them to get up and hug each other. But over the years I had learned that you can't cajole such feelings. I consoled myself that at least the process of understanding and healing had begun. The two men had taken a courageous first step, but one therapy session wasn't going to heal the hurt between them.

For Sam the road ahead would be trying. To embark on changing a relationship with a parent is like beginning a journey toward an unknown destination. It may lead to rewards and gratifications greater than ever imagined, yet it will also include danger, frustration, and disappointment along the way.

As I thought of this, I recalled my own journey with my father, which began fifteen years before. I had recently moved back to Michigan from the East to settle down, start a career, and have children.

One beautiful Sunday morning in May I piled my son, eighteen-month-old Adam, into the car and drove to Detroit to accompany my father on his annual pilgrimage to the cemetery to visit his mother's grave. With Adam in the backpack, my father and I walked through the rows of tombstones, heading toward his mother's grave. She had died when he was six years old. For the first time, he told me how his mother had died and how the family blamed his father for not providing adequate medical care for her. My father had been taken in by a loving grandmother (we visited her grave, too), who fattened him up with sweets. When she died only two years after his mother passed away, he lived with an aunt and eventually with his father and a cruel stepmother.

When I asked to see his father's grave, my father teared up. I believe this was the first time I had ever seen him cry. He explained that he had never visited his father's grave. His father had died in California thirty years before. My father had not gone to the funeral. Apparently the relationship between them had never been close. My father deeply regretted this. For him the father wound had never healed.

I feel quite strongly about the necessity for men to come to terms with their parents. I believe our experiences growing up inevitably created some loneliness and pain, but a crucial element of our existence is to provide companionship to our loved ones and to ease the pain of growth that our children are bound to experience. To do this successfully we must deal constructively and directly with our parents. We cannot rely on our wives to manage our parents. We cannot afford to avoid it, because if we have not made our peace with them before they die or become incapacitated, reconciling ourselves with the past will be that much more difficult.

More specifically, if we do not come to terms with our parents, we risk

continuing to live our lives based on our parents' expectations rather than learning what we truly desire for ourselves;

treating ourselves as we were treated as children (including shaming ourselves and inducing guilt);

feeling responsible for our parents' happiness;

continuing to blame our parents for our problems without learning to take responsibility for ourselves;

repeating dysfunctional family patterns without even realizing it;

destroying ourselves and those we love with bitterness and rage;

cutting ourselves off emotionally;

continuing to practice denial in the face of pain or dysfunction in our own lives or in the lives of our children;

losing the richness and tradition of our families, as well as an important resource at our own time of need.

I recognize that many readers do not share my enthusiasm for reconnecting with the family of origin, and for sound reasons. For those men who have been wounded through abuse or abandonment, the thought of reengaging with a parent may well seem ludicrous or even dangerous.

Others may believe that because a parent is alcoholic or mentally ill, reconnecting could injure themselves or their family. Still others, while not deeply hurt, may have found a comfortable, safe distance from their parents (or one parent) and may have no interest in getting any closer. I can readily understand such concerns, and I want these readers to know that I am not advocating reengagement if it is potentially dangerous to you or to your family. What I am suggesting is an active process of trying to understand the parent. For many this may involve a prolonged period of grieving, of getting out feelings that may have been submerged for years.

This chapter is not intended as a quick fix. The process of healing relationships with parents requires a lifetime commitment. The process, not the final destination, is the focus here. There are no easy steps to take that will result in a "cured" relationship with a parent. Rather, be prepared for an ongoing journey, where you can expect adventure, insight, disappointment, and rejuvenation along the way.

At times you will study your family like an anthropologist, seeking clues in stories and traditions. At other times you will be an emotional adventurer, saying and asking things of your family you never before dared to. The poet in you may also come out as you write down your deep feelings about your parents. So, too, the detective, as you seek the key to unlocking a family secret. You may even feel like a field general, plotting a strategy to break through your family's barriers to intimacy.

Whatever roles you play, be assured that the process will change you in significant ways.

HOW TO START UNDERSTANDING YOUR PARENTS

Your Family as a System

Most men have an overly close emotional relationship with their mothers and a more distant, less intimate, even conflictual relationship with their fathers. Why is this such a predominant pattern? To understand it, we return to the idea, first introduced in chapter 3, that we can best understand ourselves by recognizing that we grow up and exist in a family system.

Each part of the system is related to the other. For every action there is an equal and opposite reaction. When one person tries to change, as you are trying to do, the other persons are forced to change as well. This is why the task of maintaining change is most difficult within the context of your family system. Your family may not want you to change because it may force the others within the family system to change as well. Usually they do not want to change, even though you believe change would be good for them. So your family members will exert pressure on you to revert to your old ways. Remember, the person changing is almost always a threat to the fragile balances within the family.

With the onset of the men's movement, developing a closer relationship with the father has been a key focus of "men's work." Men have tried to change to be more emotionally connected with their distant fathers. But this new emphasis disrupts the whole family system. A mother might fear that her son is becoming closer to his father than to her. It is common for mothers to resist the change.

Likewise the father may feel insecure about the changes the son is trying to bring about. Many fathers have been able to maintain emotional distance by relying on their wives to manage the emotional relationships with their children. Becoming close to one of these children may seem daunting to such a stolid figure. Like the man discussed earlier in the chapter, the father may feel incapable of dealing with an emotionally close relationship with an adult child.

Roger vowed to get closer to his father, who lived several hundred miles away, by talking to his father regularly on the phone. To his dismay, after a few seconds on the phone his pop would invariably hand the phone over to his mother. His father felt uncomfortable and didn't know what to say. Mother had always been the family conversationalist.

Families often have what is called a family system triangle. This triangle serves as a distance regulator. If two people are uncomfortable with the intimacy between them, they bring a third party into their conversation to mitigate the closeness. For example, if two people are uncomfortable talking directly to each other about their own concerns, they start talking about a third person. Both can gossip, complain, or analyze the third person without having to reveal anything about themselves. This creates a pseudo-closeness between the two of them.

Pat Conroy's book and movie *The Great Santini* offers an apt illustration of how the family system triangle can operate. In one scene the teenage son is playing basketball with his father, a navy pilot who is extremely competitive and domineering. No one in the family has ever defeated

"Bull" Meachum in any game, not even at checkers. With the whole family watching, the son finally puts the winning lay-up past his father. Bull is so enraged that he claims his son didn't win, because "you've got to win by two."

The mother takes great satisfaction in her son's victory. She herself has never been able to "win" with Bull, so when her son wins, it feels like her victory, too. More important, it signifies that her eldest boy will not be prevented by the heavy-handed father from becoming a man in his own right. She tries therefore to defend her son from Bull by arguing that Bull has just invented the two-point rule. This only enrages him more, and he shoves her out of the way.

Now it is the son's turn to react in the triangle. He tries to defend his beloved mother from the bullish father. This is a role he, like many eldest sons, has played regularly. Bull then calls his son a sissy for not wanting to compete any longer and for defending his mother. As the son walks defiantly up the stairs to his room, his father bounces the basketball off his head. "Go ahead. Cry, baby, cry," he says.

Shortly thereafter, as the son lies in his bed, the mother comes in to excuse the father's behavior. She explains that that was his father's peculiar manner of showing his son he respected him. She points outside, where the father is still shooting baskets in the rainy dusk. "He does what he does because he loves you, Ben. . . . That's the only way he knows how to say I'm sorry . . . and let me tell you there isn't another person in God's world that he would do that for. . . . You try to think of that when you feel he doesn't love you."

What is the son to think? How is he to feel? His family is a confusing and emotionally draining system. If he supports his mother, his father becomes incensed. If his father hurts him, his mother excuses the father's behavior. How, as an adult, will he be able to come to terms with such a tangled situation?

A crucial exercise I prescribe for the men I work with is to describe the basic triangle in their families of origin. (The notion of a triangle is based on the teachings of Murray Bowen, one of the pioneers of family therapy. It was also popularized by Harriet Lerner in *The Dance of Anger*.) Most often the triangle consists of mother, father, and child. But other triangles can exist that wield equal influence. Let me describe some triangles of men I've worked with.

Vic felt close to his mother. As the eldest child, he felt he had to keep her company and cheer up her otherwise drab existence with an emotionally distant father. His father then began to taunt him for preferring to be around the house and "womenfolk" rather than with him at the family-owned garage. In analyzing the relationship now as an adult, Vic thinks his father was jealous of his closeness with his mother, who perhaps was using Vic as a substitute husband.

Ray grew up feeling sorry for his father, who worked especially hard. With his parents constantly arguing about money, Ray felt that each parent was trying to draw him into an alliance against the other. When Ray sided with his father, his mother accused him of not loving her, as if it was possible to love only one parent. When he sided with his mother, he felt the pain of his father's rejection.

Years after childhood, Ken was still bitter toward his mother. She had been the catalyst for countless beatings by informing his father about Ken's wrongdoings each day. Even though she knew that "when your father gets home" he would go out of control, she fed the conspiracy.

As an adult, Ken realized his mother had no control over him or the other children, so she used the threat of his father's beatings to borrow control.

Andy, the youngest of three children, grew up in a house with his mother and grandmother. The two women had a very competitive and contentious relationship. In therapy years later, Andy realized that he had been a pawn in their battles, with each trying to show the other that she could be a better mother to Andy. This made Andy feel guilty much of the time because if he pleased one woman, he automatically seemed to displease the another.

Here are some ways to identify a triangle (from Emily Marlin's *Genograms*).

You are in a triangle if

> you have a very strong reaction to one person and turn to another for support, comfort, and reassurance;
>
> you experience strong feelings (especially anger, guilt, shame, or fear) often associated with triangles;
>
> you are overinvolved in trying to fix one person's problems;
>
> you can use words such as fixer, rescuer, or buffer to describe your role.

Take a moment to think about yourself and your family of origin in terms of triangles. In your journal describe the essential triangles that continue to influence your life. Once you have described your essential triangles, become aware of how you feel when you are stuck in one. If you wish to disengage, start with one simple rule: Refuse to discuss one family member's problems with another.

Rather than trying to fix the problems between two other people, encourage them to work them out on their own.

Family Secrets and Forbidden Topics

Another crucial dimension in understanding your family is learning the patterns of family secrets and forbidden topics. Toxic events and themes in families over the generations are made even more powerful and threatening because they have been turned into secrets, denied, or otherwise deemed off-limits for discussion.

Since most of these secrets involve covering up something the family is ashamed of, the family member who inquires about them meets tremendous resistance to his efforts to learn the truth. Among the most common examples of topics that are kept secret are addiction, suicide, illegitimacy, adoption, mental illness, incest, and affairs.

Denial is one of the ways a family copes with secrecy. The denial of one secret spreads to denial in other areas, thus stifling honest communication within the family. Keeping certain subjects secret also increases the chance that family members will engage in similar behaviors in future generations. Another ill effect of secrecy is its tendency to so distort reality that family members feel insecure or "crazy." This is the uneasy sense of knowing that something is wrong but being prevented from asking about it or being lied to when an inquiry is made. One then begins to doubt one's own reality and perceptions.

A central strategy for coming to terms with your family is to open up the secrecy by mentioning or inquiring about the forbidden topic during one-to-one conversations with family members, when they might be more receptive.

Dennis had suspicions about his parentage. From the time he was a teenager, he heard rumors that the man he thought was his father was not his true father. Once, when he was thirteen, he overheard a conversation between his mother and his aunt that made him suspicious. He was too fearful at the time to ask for clarification. Years later his sister-in-law told his wife that she, too, had heard rumors about Dennis's parentage. When his wife told him, Dennis still maintained denial, dismissing the story as rumor.

When Dennis and his wife went for counseling, the question again surfaced. The therapist was particularly intrigued by the rumor because he saw a possible connection between this family secret and Dennis's own withdrawal from his wife, which had created conflict in their marriage.

After much support and coaxing, Dennis was persuaded to ask his mother about the rumor. Without any hesitation she confirmed it. Dennis indeed had been adopted by his current father when he was four. His natural father had divorced his mother after he returned from the war and had agreed to allow the second husband to adopt Dennis. Even more shocking, his biological father lived only a few miles from where Dennis had grown up.

Several months later, with the support of his men's group, Dennis set up a meeting with his father. He told Dennis that he had stayed out of his life to make it easier for Dennis, so he "wouldn't have to struggle with two fathers." He had always kept track of Dennis. He knew of his many professional successes and was proud of him.

What amazed Dennis about the experience was the startling similarities he found between himself and his father. Finally, after many years of struggle, he was able truly to understand where he was coming from.

Other men in my groups have also confronted secrets. Jerry, for instance, asked his rabbi father about the discrepancy between his birth date and his parents' anniversary date. The father confessed that Jerry had been conceived before he and his wife were married. Joe, who had lost his father when Joe was seven, asked his sister to explain their father's death. She confirmed his suspicions — his father had died from cirrhosis of the liver, not liver cancer as he had been told. He was a severe alcoholic, not the saint that Joe's mother always told him he was. When Ted confided in his father that he was having an affair, his father shared with him for the first time that he, too, had had affairs throughout his marriage.

Like so many others, these men found great relief in having the family secrets revealed. Secrets cause us to live in denial and shame. The truth enables us to find dignity and peace.

Think about the secrets and denial that might exist in your own family of origin. Focus on subjects that are considered strictly taboo. Write down these forbidden topics or questions about your family that never seem to be answered adequately.

What are your suspicions?

Why are you afraid to inquire? What is the worst possible answer? What do you fear will happen if you broach the topic?

Who might have information which could help you?

Can you devise a plan to open up this shadowy area?

What support do you need to commence this process?

Who can you enlist to support you?

Getting to Know Each Parent on a One-to-One Basis.

Once you begin to understand yourself in the context of your family system, you can move from this cognitive understanding to a more personal relationship with each parent. The triangles and family secrets that we just discussed present obstacles for us in moving toward a closer, individual relationship with each parent. This is why it is so crucial to be aware of those two aspects of family functioning.

The key to developing one-to-one relationships with family members is to spend time alone with each of them. This requires planning ways to be with one parent without having the other around. Most often the father is the elusive one. As discussed earlier, fathers usually rely on their wives to negotiate relationships with their offspring. So it is particularly important to devise strategies for spending time alone with him. (And alone means without your spouse. You, not your spouse, are responsible for your relationship with your parents.)

Here are some suggestions for developing one-to-one relationships.

- Join each parent in an activity that he or she enjoys. For a father this usually involves sports: fishing, bowling, golf, or spectator sports. For a mother this may mean taking her to the theater or a concert or just going out to lunch. The crucial thing is to do the activity alone with each parent.

- If you live near a parent, consider setting up regular dates to get together. You might go out for breakfast, lunch, or dinner monthly (or even weekly); get season tickets together (sports or a concert series); or work on a project together. By being a regular part of the schedule, the date is more likely to actually happen.

- If you live some distance away, plan to spend some alone time with each parent on your trips. Let them know well before you arrive of your intention, and when you talk to them on the phone, always talk to each separately. Three-way calls inhibit meaningful conversation.

Listening to Your Parents' Story

Asking your parents about the stories of their lives can be the most useful step in making peace with them. Especially important is learning the story of their own experience growing up in their families of origin. By asking about their families of origin, you gain an intergenerational perspective. Behavior that may not have made sense to you in your own childhood may suddenly make perfect sense if put in the context of another generation. Roy, for instance, was always confused about the way his father responded to Roy's mother's excessive concern about her health. Rather than taking a firm stand with her or suggesting that she seek counseling, his father would take her from doctor to doctor.

When Roy took the step of asking his father about his family history, his father's behavior suddenly made perfect sense. Roy's father told him that when he was a young boy, his own mother became ill. Roy's grandfather did not believe that his wife was seriously ill. He hesitated to spend money to take her to the doctor. When she died from the illness, Roy's grandfather was blamed for neglecting her and was shunned by her family for the rest of his life.

Suddenly Roy understood why his father made it a priority to attend to his wife's medical needs. His father would not risk repeating his own father's perceived neglect. This insight was a great source of relief to Roy and enabled him to understand and forgive.

Presented here are some suggestions for eliciting your parents' life stories.

1. Inform each parent of your desire to learn more about his or her life history. Ask if he or she would be willing to find some time to begin the process.

2. Conduct each discussion separately. Try to avoid a triangle where one parent is disagreeing with the other about family history.

3. Do a family tree with each parent. Using a large pad, some markers, and a tape recorder, sit down with each parent and sketch out a three-generation family tree. In family therapy we call this document a genogram. A tape recorder helps capture the richness of your parents' stories, for you and the next generations to enjoy later.

4. Use photographs and old home movies to encourage your parents to talk to you about their family

stories. In a wonderful book titled *Family Tales, Family Wisdom*, Robert Akeret describes a ten-step "Elder Tale Program" for using photos to elicit your parents' stories. He suggest that you ask your parents to select photos from various periods of their lives to help them in describing their stories. Set a series of dates with them to go over photos from each period. He also suggests that you ask your parent to describe a single day from his or her youth, a key turning point, the high and the low points, and influential people or experiences.

5. Take your parent on a visit to significant places in his or her life. Earlier I described my experience of going to the family cemetery with my father. Taking a trip or making a visit (again, just the two of you) can be a transforming experience in your relationship with your parent. You might visit the places where your parent lived while growing up, the homes and neighborhoods where you were raised, the family cemetery, or a place where the parent vacationed in youth. (You might want to bring along a camera or a video recorder for future generations.)

It is best to keep this journey brief and focused. This is intended to be not an extended vacation with your parent, but merely one way to elicit his or her life story — and in doing so, part of your own.

SPECIAL ISSUES WITH FATHERS

The issues involved in trying to heal your relationship with your parents are different for fathers and mothers.

There are several reasons why most men have the greatest difficulty coming to terms with the father.

Competition

Competition between father and son is the most significant obstacle to resolving the father-son conflict. When a son is born, the competition begins with the attention of the female (the wife and mother) as the object. Even when the father sincerely wants to have a son, he inevitably finds himself at least partially jealous of all the attention the child is receiving from the mother. This is also true with daughters, but the feelings are more intense with the son because he, too, is a male, and the father has been conditioned for his entire life to be competitive with other males.

As the child grows older, the competition becomes two way and intensifies. The son learns to compete with the father for the mother's attention and affection. This is particularly true if the mother is the sole or primary childcare giver. In families where the father provides direct care for the children, the competition lessens because the son receives nurturing from the father without having to compete for it.

Most sons also compete with the work environment for their fathers' attention. The father is not with the child because he is at work, or his disposition is grouchy because he has had a bad day at the office.

As a boy reaches adolescence, the competition escalates. Now the child becomes a physical threat to the father. He is bigger, stronger, faster. The father, as a male, has difficulty not feeling competitive with another male who may dwarf him in size or physical strength. So even though the father may take pride in his son's becoming a man, a part of him is also threatened by this.

As the son embarks on a career, competition with his father becomes an even more significant factor. If the father is highly successful in the work world, the son feels the pressure to match or exceed the father's status. If the father has been relatively unsuccessful, the son may curtail his ambition lest he aggravate the father by showing him up. Or he may feel excessive pressure because his father wants so much for him to succeed.

I often hear men admit that they feel like they are trying to succeed for two. Their striving is not so much for themselves as for their fathers, who may have failed to obtain their goals in life. This common scenario, of living vicariously through the son's success, places tremendous pressure on the son.

In your journal you may want to list all the ways you have felt competitive with your father at different times in your life, from childhood, adolescence, and young adulthood. Do you still feel in competition with him? You may feel this way even if he is deceased. These are ways the competition may have manifested itself:

- a sense of never being able to please him;

- a sense of being driven to do better than he did—in your career, making money, as a husband, as a parent, or in an avocation (sports, hobbies, etc.);

- wanting to show him up;

- trying to be a better son to your mother than he was a husband to her.

After completing your list, talk openly to your father about your competitive feelings toward him. Tell him you would like to get to know him better but that the competition gets in the way. Finally, simply quit competing with him. Declare the contest over. It takes two, and if you bow out, the game is essentially up.

Several men in my therapy groups have tried to end their competitive relationships with their fathers. Wayne's competition with his father centered around his mother. His father believed that each favored the other over him. Whenever Wayne spent time with his mother, his father took it as a personal affront. The rivalry intensified after Wayne's parents divorced when he was in high school. The situation was particularly painful to Wayne's father because his wife had left him for another man. Wayne would lie to his father to conceal his visits to his mother.

After years of frustration, Wayne, at the urging of his men's group, decided to talk honestly to his father about how he felt. He carefully planned the talk, not as an attack on his father but as a true expression of his frustration. He was not blaming but explaining his own pain honestly.

To his surprise and delight, his father was able to hear him without becoming defensive. His father was able to open up to Wayne for the first time about how devastated he had been by his wife's betrayal. It was her, not Wayne, with whom he remained angry. After that talk Wayne no longer had to lie to his father, the first step in a vastly improved relationship between the two men.

Chet, a thirty-four-year-old electronics whiz, was the son of an electrician who always dreamed of becoming an inventor. With his father's support Chet had set up a small electronics firm after graduating from college. It was a hardscrabble business for Chet, who found himself constantly struggling to keep his firm afloat. In therapy Chet questioned whether he really wanted to be in business for himself or whether he was trying to fulfill his father's dream. Chet realized that he was more inclined to be an artist than a businessman, but felt compelled to continue in business.

Once again at the group's urging, Chet talked to his father about his dilemma. The most important part of the conversation for Chet was admitting to his father his own reluctance about the career, which his father had picked for him. Even though his father denied any ulterior motive, Chet found the clearing so liberating that he was able to give up the business world and go to art school.

Unexpressive Fathers

One of the few things more uncomfortable than competing with a father is being ignored by him. Someone once said that the opposite of love is indifference. Indifferent fathers are emotionally withdrawn. They are so closed emotionally that they appear incapable of demonstrating love to their children. Some are workaholics, some are alcoholics or display other addictive or compulsive behaviors, others are just cold and aloof. They rarely attend to their sons' activities, play games with them, or initiate conversation. Instead they spend their time working, watching TV, reading the paper, or drinking until they fall asleep.

Many of these men have such grumpy dispositions that any interaction with their children tends to be unpleasant. A conspiracy of sorts may exist between the mother and her children to let the sleeping dog lie. Waking it up only results in snarling.

My professional experience indicates that the indifferent father is often a depressed father. He tends to be a man who is so burdened by his own worries or so stressed by his work situation that he has nothing left to give when he returns home. For several reasons the depression in these men is not easy to recognize: men aren't supposed to get depressed; they often relieve their depression through "self-medication"; and they express themselves with anger rather than sadness.

Not all indifferent fathers are depressed, of course. Some just do not know how to deal with children or don't believe a father should get involved with kids. Still others were raised in abusive situations and have vowed not to be hurtful to their children. Knowing no alternative, they simply withdraw to avoid abusing their own children.

Adult sons of indifferent fathers frequently grow so frustrated trying to get their fathers' attention that they quit trying. I have found it quite difficult to motivate these men to try once again to connect with their fathers. They have inoculated themselves against the pain of rejection by writing off their fathers and limiting contact with them to obligatory occasions. If they have any contact at all with their parents, it is probably through their mothers.

If you believe your father was an indifferent father, I urge you to try once more to reconnect. If your father dies before you do, he will always remain in your mind an uncaring man who did not love you. The question of love is the central one for the children of such men. A man may infer that his father loved him; his mother may assure him that his father loved him, even friends or other relatives may vouch for his father's devotion. But unless a man hears it directly from his father, he can never be sure.

When Lenny's father had a heart attack at age seventy-four, Lenny initially resisted the idea of flying south to be with his father. Recognizing that it might have been now or never, however, he took the risk, took time off work, and spent the next six days at his father's bedside. When he returned to the group, Lenny told the following story about his father.

"As I was visiting him in the hospital, he started feeling my shirt and wanted to know where I had gotten my shirt. I said 'Well, Banana Republic,' and then he started feeling my pants and wanted to know where I had gotten my pants. I said 'JC Penney, and then he started feeling my tie and wanted to know where I had gotten my tie. I was thinking. What's wrong with this man? He had had a heart attack, not a stroke. It shouldn't be affecting his brain. But then I realized that he wanted to touch me, and he didn't know how. I held his hand, and I got choked up, as I'm doing now. I was thirty, but we had never told each other we loved each other, and we had never held hands or touched each other like that. It was a very painful moment, but it took me beyond that because I've done those things with him now; and when he passes away, it's going to be hard, but I think I can live with that."

Something shifted when Lenny became the caretaker for his father. For the first time Lenny was able to see previously concealed facets of his father: vulnerability, fear, neediness, and the capacity to love. At the end of the week Lenny's father kissed and hugged him. He thanked him for coming. He told Lenny to tell his own children every day that their father loves them. His father even said that his dog, Spider, loved Lenny. Though Lenny didn't hear the three magic words directly, for him this was enough.

Sid decided to write letters to his father. Here is the first one.

Dear Dad,

How are you? I'm sitting at a cafeteria eating a burger and fries for lunch. Work is going okay, considering the down economy.

The kids are both doing very well. I'll be coaching Billy's little league baseball team this summer.

The largest reason for my writing you today stems from discussions at my men's group last Tuesday night. The group consists of seven guys including the official therapist. Last week one of the guys talked about his father, who had just passed away. He is the only one in the group who has lost his father. The majority of our conversations were about our fathers. It seems that guys have many issues with their dads. I've never yet heard one of the guys talking about their relationships with their moms.

I guess we relate to our dads or at least significant males in our lives. Listening to a couple of the guys talk about their dads was very interesting. A couple of the guys have alcoholic dads that have been or are physically or verbally abusive.

It seems to me that no matter what we've all received from our dads, there is still something else we would have liked. When I think of my childhood, there are certain things I would like to have received. I'm not referring to material things, but emotional involvement, support, etc. I am in no way trying to criticize you as a father. In actuality, I want to thank you for all the good things you've done for me. You don't drink, you don't smoke and I don't recall you being abusive. I am thankful for having a dad like you. You worked hard, were self-reliant and responsible. So, there may be things I wish I could have received and I'm sure Billy will someday tell me he wished I could have given him something more. I'm working hard to be the best father I can be. I just wanted you to know that I Love You. I have many fond memories of doing things with my dad. You're a good man and I have tremendous respect for you. Thanks for being as good a dad as you were and continue to be.

I love you. Your son,

Sid

To his surprise his father wrote back. The letter was stiff and impersonal, but he closed with "I've always loved you." Seeing these words was a turning point for Sid.

Domineering Fathers

An authoritarian father can present another obstacle to attempts to heal relationships. Domination was the old-world approach to parenting. It displayed itself in a wide range of behavior, from emotional coercion to physical abuse. Fatherhood meant being dominant, tough, and uncompromising toward children. Many of these fathers subscribed to the "Spare the rod, spoil the child" maxim, and all believed that if they went easy on a boy, he would turn out to be a sissy.

Many men seeking counseling were raised in homes where physical punishment was the norm, usually delivered by the father. Only recently have we begun to recognize how pervasive physical punishment is in American families and how destructive it has been to our society.

In his important book *Spare the Child*, Philip Grevin traces the roots of physical punishment to the religious

traditions of Western society. "Although many generations, quoting the Bible, have insisted that 'the rod' is a
necessity in raising children, physical punishment from
the mildest to the most severe forms a continuum of violence that needs to be scrutinized, understood, and abandoned as the ordinary way of disciplining children."

Among the psychological and social problems that
can frequently be traced to childhood physical punishment are anxiety, hostility, insensitivity, depression, rigid-
ity, dissociation, and the notion that we can best protect
our loved ones by destroying their will.

I do not intend to turn this chapter into a moral or
philosophical treatise on punishment. I hope I am clear in
my conviction that physical punishment — or even an
uncompromising stance — is harmful. What I hope to do
in this chapter is to address the concerns of the men who
were raised in this manner by their parents. How do they
deal with their parents and the question of forgiveness as
adults? Perhaps most important, how do they avoid treating their children abusively and discover new, more positive means of parenting?

Many of the answers are addressed elsewhere in the
book. What follows is a more specific guide to coming to
terms with domineering or abusive parents.

1. *Address the feelings of rage about abusive treatment.*
Victims of abuse rage about their mistreatment. For some
the rage may come out directly in anger toward a parent.
For others the rage may come out sideways — as anger
toward people in general, toward their children, or toward
situations. People describe these men as having "an edge"
or "a quick trigger."

The first step in healing usually involves uncovering this rage and finding safe and appropriate outlets for it. For most men this means working with a therapist or with a men's group to be able safely to remember and describe their experiences.

2. *Work through these feelings.* How so? A variety of approaches are useful: (a) talking about it to others; (b) writing about it in a journal; (c) drawing or finding some other artistic means to express feelings; (d) finding a safe form of physical expression of the feelings — exercise, sports, a martial art, yoga, or meditation.

3. *Understand the roots of the abuse.* To accomplish this part of the process a man needs to learn his father's story, the steps for which were outlined in an earlier part of this chapter. Embedded in the story of a man who abuses is usually the saga of a boy who was abused in his early years.

4. *After working on the first three steps, consider the question of forgiveness.* Forgiveness is perhaps the most complicated of issues when it comes to dealing with parents. Sometimes men tell me that they have forgiven their parents, but actually they have not done the emotional work necessary for true forgiveness to occur. Forgiveness is not an intellectual concept but an emotional process. One cannot merely think one's way to forgiveness; one must go through the grief and rage that inevitably result from abuse.

I do believe that working on forgiveness is essential to discovering one's true self. This does not necessarily mean that one has to forgive, but one does need to weigh the question of what it would take to forgive. Is it necessary for the parent to admit the abuse? Must the parent apologize? Does a man seek understanding or revenge? Does one blame himself for having been abused because he was a "bad boy"?

To be honest, I must report that most abused men I have worked with have not found peace with the abuser. Many fathers who were abusive when they were younger continue to be authoritarian and domineering now when they are older. They tend not to be any easier to get along with as old men, even though they may have lost their physical strength.

What the adult sons of abusive fathers have been able to find is more peace within themselves. Through therapy, group work, and their own personal exploration, many important changes take place that enable them to feel better about themselves.

Doug, a thirty-eight-year-old businessman who was abused by his father, talked to several of his siblings about the abuse they had all received. Through these conversations he was able to realize that he had been abused not because of something bad about him or something he had done. Rather a portrait emerged of systematic abuse by both parents, whom he learned were abused themselves as children. For Doug the most important moment of personal change was when he took down the paddle, which had been hanging on the kitchen wall, and told his six- and eight-year-old sons that he was no longer going to use physical punishment as a means of discipline.

Ted, a forty-three-year-old artist, grew up with a father who became abusive when he drank. Once his father stopped the drinking and had started attending Alcoholics Anonymous meetings, Ted felt safe to begin a normal relationship with him. He started playing golf on a regular basis with his father. Ted found additional comfort by attending Adult Children of Alcoholics meetings, where for the first time he was able to tell the story of growing up in an alcoholic family to people who understood and listened. Through the group he also learned strategies for avoiding his father if he started drinking again.

I want to reemphasize the importance of getting help if you were raised in an abusive family. Abuse leaves scars. If unattended to, denied, or ignored, these scars continue to cause pain. Such wounds can open up at unexpected times, hurting the people you least want to hurt.

I also encourage you to do your emotional work as soon as possible. Perhaps because anger takes its toll on the cardiovascular system, in my clinical experience I find that abusive fathers die relatively young.

Deceased Fathers

Just because a father has died does not mean that one's emotional work with that father is complete. Because men often do not know how to grieve, losing our fathers leaves us with unhealed wounds.

John's father died at age thirty-five, when John was a boy of seven. When John was thirty-four, he dreamed that he himself died. "I had just turned thirty-five in the dream — my father's age when he died — and was in a car accident and died, exactly the way he died. It was sort of a meaningless accident. I was just driving along using good rules of the road and wearing my seat belt and driving safely, and I was hit by someone else and died instantly.

"It wasn't like the other dreams I have had about death. It was a very calm dream. I felt very calm and very free. It felt like I had been liberated somehow. I felt like I didn't have to go through all the stuff that I've had to go through for the last two months. I felt relief that I didn't have to work two jobs anymore. I felt relief that I didn't have to fight with my wife anymore. I didn't have to live in fear of dying, because I was dead, and that was a relief, too. I didn't have to live in fear of dying like my father at thirty-five, because it had already happened, and I was now free of that.

"So when I woke up I felt really great. Like I said before, the dream was not very vivid, but as the days went on it became more vivid in my head, and I could remember more details of it. But I interpreted it as being liberated from the idea of having to be like my father, having to work like my father. I felt like having that dream was a milestone in my life because I had had it without all the stress usually associated with bad dreams like that."

The dream so stirred John that he decided to take a trip to visit his father's grave. The visit became a ritual of healing. His father was buried in a mausoleum, which had been unattended for many years. When John arrived, he spent an entire afternoon cleaning the tiles, planting flowers, and contemplating his memories of his father. He brought back rocks from the earth, which he placed on his desk at work. He built a shadow box, filled with mementos of his father, which he showed to his children.

For John the completion of the grieving process had been stalled for twenty-seven years. At last John felt freed from the legacy of his father, free to pursue his own life as he saw fit.

Another member of the group, Bob, had also lost his father. But in Bob's case the pain was even more severe because after his parents' divorce his father had abandoned the family. After his twelfth birthday, Bob never saw his father again. At the urging of the group Bob began a search to learn about his father. "All I knew about him was that he lived in Chicago, and had been a physician there, and that was about it. I also knew that my aunt (my mother's sister) had some friends who were his patients. So even though I had never really talked to her before about it, I called her. She gave me these people's names. I called them; they gave me some information about him and some more names. Before long I had talked to twenty or thirty people who knew him. I eventually found his second wife and her daughter and my uncle, his brother.

"It was a little scary. Just as people would start describing him, I'd think, This is getting a little too close to home here. It was a really emotional thing for me, and as I started to think more and more about it, I realized that I had lived most of my life thinking of myself as fatherless. I remember feeling like all of a sudden there was this big shadow over me that had been there all along but I had really never turned around to look at it.

"It changed the way I viewed myself. It didn't solve my problems, it didn't make me a new person. To the contrary, it made me more the person that I really was. It let me accept myself more than I ever had before. I think that it was almost like a script that I was unconsciously playing out. If I'm not aware of it, it can have a lot of control over what I'm doing."

After this search Bob wrote the following letter to his father who had been dead for twelve years:

Dear Dad,

Well, it's 25 years later and here I am finally writing to you. It feels strange to write "Dear Dad" — I never have, now that I think about it. I can't even remember what I used to call you — Dad? Daddy? Pop?

As I write this there are tears in my eyes. Because I never knew you. Because you left me. Because I never had my father in my life. Because I didn't get a chance to know you. Because you died before I could find you. And because you never found me.

It may sound hard to believe, but I went 25 years before I really let myself think of myself as "having a father." Somehow I managed to grow up without one, and at the same time convince myself that that was ok — "no big deal," you know — "everyone's parents get divorced," right? But in the last three months all that's changed. Because for the first time in 25 years I am getting to know you.

You know, Dad, I'm really not mad that you left — I just DON'T UNDERSTAND IT. I don't understand why you left me behind. And you did leave me — your son, who was (and is) a part of YOU — behind to deal with what you couldn't deal with. Not very fair. I really don't understand it. Didn't you want to know me? Didn't you like me? Didn't you see that if you couldn't deal with it that it would be hard for me too? Why did you leave?

You know, Dad, I worked so hard at denying your existence — with a lot of help from Mom, and from all the other assorted relatives who never talked about you, and from you, too, now that I think about it — that I never even saw a picture of you until this past summer. For years I just went around with some really vague recollection of what you looked like — black glasses, purple shirts, Lucky Strikes. I remember so little.

Looking at pictures for the first time, I've started to see you as a real person, not just as a vague and distant memory, eroded by years of blocking, pretending, and projecting. When I see the pictures of you and me on the beach together, I look SO happy. You know, I can't remember ever feeling that happy. But you look happy too.

. . . I mean what was it like to be my father? Did you love me when I was little? You must have. But if you did, why did you leave me?

Hey, I gotta go now. I'll write more. You can write back if you want. Actually, you can't, because you're dead. But I wish you could. I loved you. And I still love you.

Bob

P.S. The Bears won today. You would have been happy. We could have gone to the games together, you know?

MEN AND MOTHERS

If we fail to know our mothers, can we truly know other women? If we struggle all our lives to separate from our mothers, can we ever accept the more feminine parts of ourselves? If we never allow ourselves to feel our mothers' pain, can we ever feel our own?

In a powerful scene in "Roots," fourteen-year-old Kunte Kinte returns to his parents' hut in Gambia after spending several weeks in the woods being initiated into manhood by the male elders of his tribe. His entrance to the hut is blocked by his mother, whom he has not seen for several weeks. As she stands outside the hut, she informs him that he cannot enter. "You do not live here anymore," she tells him. "Your father has built for you your own hut and you must now go live there."

Kunte Kinte, trying to look brave, is stunned and hurt. After weeks in the woods, he wants his mother's comfort, her food, the safety of her hut. She, too, does not feel as strong as her actions indicate. She knows she must tell him to go, but she wants to hold on to him, to protect him from the dangers of manhood.

For several seconds they look at each other. Suddenly, both with tears in their eyes, she reaches out for him, and the scene ends with their long embrace. In the next scene

Kunte Kinte, while away from the village searching for a log to use to make a drum for his brother, is captured by slave hunters. He and his mother never see or hear from each other again.

These two emotional scenes epitomize the essential dilemma mothers and sons face. The mother knows her son must separate from her to be able to forge his masculine identity. Yet she knows as she pushes him out of the nest that he will be entering the dangerous, unpredictable world. Likewise the son, who enjoys the safety and comfort of his mother and her world, recognizes that to prove himself a man he must leave her and enter the scary, challenging realm of the outside world.

This is an experience I know all too well. I grew up with two mothers, my real mother and my maternal grandmother. Men were there, too, but my father and grandfather were almost always at work. At least three quarters of my waking hours were spent in the women's world.

I can remember struggles with these caring women beginning when I was in second or third grade. I wanted to ride my bike several blocks away to go to Putski's party store; they were afraid to let me cross the busy street. I wanted to play hockey; they were afraid I'd break my bones. I wanted to stay out after dark talking to my friends at the park; they wanted me home.

Most men can rewrite my story with their own script. Much of our lives have been spent trying to separate ourselves from our mother's world. For many the struggle continues well into adulthood:

- Lee's mother gets upset because he won't wear a sport coat and tie to church. She believes that as a respected lawyer in the community, he should carry himself with more dignity. So for his forty-fifth birthday, she buys him two sport coats and several ties.

• Joe has a crisis when his wife leaves him for another man. To be "helpful" his mother brings him dinner every night for several months and stays around to be sure he's OK.

• When Ronald's father leaves his mother, she leans on her fourteen-year-old-son for her principal support. Every night she insists that he sit with her at the darkened kitchen table as she sips sherry and tells him about her sorrows.

• Dwayne desperately wants to leave medicine. He feels burned out as a physician. Yet to do so would greatly disappoint his mother, a nurse, who always encouraged her only son to become a doctor. He fears that if he left, "it might kill her."

These patterns of the overinvolved mother are quite familiar to all of us. The stories have become so common that they are often clichés, the stuff TV sitcoms are made of. "Mama's boy" is a familiar phrase that every American male has probably worked hard to avoid.

Yet for the men still trying to figure out how to disentangle successfully from their mothers without destroying the relationship, the psychological issues are quite real. The trick is to set up the boundaries that are firm enough to prevent your mother's unwanted intrusions into your life yet permeable enough to allow a caring, mutually satisfying relationship with her.

Here are some guidelines that have proved useful in this endeavor.

1. *Get to know your mother better.*   I know I've said this before, and you're probably thinking I really don't understand. Many men fear that if they spend time getting to know them, their mothers will take it as an opportunity to start running their lives.

But my point here is that many men have been so busy trying to keep their mothers at bay that they have never really taken the time to get to know them. Because we are male and our mothers are female (as well as being our mothers), we do not know and do not understand the intricacies of their personalities and their lives. We tend to know only one dimension of them, the maternal one.

How can you begin to learn more about her as a total person? Ask about her experiences before she became a mother. What was her life like as a girl, as an adolescent, as a young adult before she had children? Was her dream always to have a family, or did she have other hopes and aspirations that were thwarted because she lived at a time when opportunities for women were limited?

Ask about her experience as a mother. What was difficult about it for her? Which parts did she enjoy? Which parts did she detest. Does she have regrets, disappointments? Did she wish she could have spent her time doing something else? What is she most proud of? What was it like to raise a boy?

You can even ask about her opinion of feminism and the women's movement? Was she ever a victim of discrimination or harassment?

Ask her about her experience of your current relationship with her. What more would she like from the relationship? How does she experience you? What obstacles does she believe impede your relationship together? What would she most like to be different about the relationship?

2. *Clearly state how you would like your relationship with your mother to be.* Many men define their relationships with their mothers in negative terms. If they experience their mothers as too intrusive, they feel like they are constantly pushing their mothers away. This is negative, defining the relationship in terms of what they do not want.

The real challenge is to allow yourself to imagine in positive terms what type of relationship you would like with your mother. If you could change the relationship, how would it be different? How could your mother be a resource for you? Under what circumstances could you more enjoy your mother? What would you like to be able to discuss with her that you currently cannot?

3. *Take responsibility for your own part in blocking the development of the relationship.* What unfinished business do you have with your mother? What have you been unable to say to her that you wish you could say? What obstacles do you put in the way of developing a better relationship?

If you find yourself angry at your mother, it is your responsibility to figure out why and to try to do something about your feelings. Write about it. Talk to a sibling, a friend, a therapist, or a support group. Try to see her side of the story. One thing is clear: If you hold on to your anger toward your mother, it will inevitably work its way into your relationship with other females, whether your mate, your daughter, or a co-worker.

Men with Distant or Emotionally Unavailable Mothers

Not all men experience too much intrusiveness from their mothers. Many men in my practice describe their mothers as emotionally distant or unavailable. For the most part these mothers were either so overwhelmed by the burdens of motherhood that they could not function adequately in the role; had emotional or substance abuse; or did not buy into society's notion of a mother as a self-sacrificing slave.

In many instances these mothers were the casualties of the discrimination against women that was so dominant yet hidden in the 1950s, 1960s, and 1970s. They were expected to look neat and trim, to raise the children cheerfully on their own, to give up career aspirations, and to be dutiful and devoted to their husbands. The notion of themselves as people with their own needs was unthinkable. Many women could not— or chose not to— live up to these unrealistic expectations.

Reed's mother raised eight children in near poverty. She never had time to tend to Reed's emotional needs or to those of any other children. She was too busy cooking, washing, and helping out with the small family farm.

Glen's mother spent most of her time reading novels, while Glen's father was away at work building the family business. Only in later years did Glen realize that his mother had been addicted to tranquilizers during most of those years. Furthermore, until he began asking his mother about her history, Glen did not know that she had been sexually abused by an uncle when she was a girl.

Hugh's mother was mean and cruel to him and his siblings. She didn't really seem to want to be a mother. In interviewing his mother about her life, Hugh discovered that she had never wanted to marry his father but had been forced into it by her own parents when she became pregnant at age eighteen. Although he knew that his father could be cruel, too, he hadn't remembered until talking to his sister that his father regularly beat his mother. Evidently Hugh had repressed the memory.

Troy's mother (and father) worked from the time he was young. As the eldest child, from the time he was ten he was expected to look after his younger siblings. After his parents divorced, his mother set no limits on him. He was allowed to do virtually whatever he wanted. Not until his own marriage began to fall apart because he was having an affair with an older woman did Troy recognize that he was still wanting a woman to set limits on him. He had not learned how to set limits for himself.

Herb's mother abandoned the family when he was twelve. For many years the only time Herb would see his mother was at Christmas or sometimes on his birthday. His humiliation was extreme. All the other children he knew had mothers. No one had explained to him why she had gone away, so he blamed himself for her leaving. He assumed it was because he had been disobedient and had made her life hard.

As an adult in therapy Herb tried to work through his feelings of abandonment. At one level he was full of rage toward her. Yet another part of him wanted to reconcile with her. There was even a part of him that longed to protect her, to take care of her, to provide for her, to rescue her from the dire circumstances she was living in.

Herb had difficulty understanding and reconciling such diffuse feelings. After helping him sort out his feelings, I suggested that Herb begin to reconnect with his mother through letters. Phone calls were too painful; each time he called, his mother would describe her awful circumstances.

Through the letters Herb was able to begin a meaningful dialogue with his mother. He described to her how he felt, and she began to tell him her story. She did not make excuses, nor did she deny what she had done. She explained that she had felt totally inadequate as a mother and had been more interested in men and fun than she was in parenting. She felt terribly guilty about this. Rather than continuing to be an ineffectual mother, she left the children to their father, who was in her opinion a much better parent.

Herb was not happy with the explanation, but he appreciated her frankness. Even though the letters did not heal the relationship, he felt better learning that at least he had not been to blame for her leaving. The dialogue begun in the letters raised Herb's hopes for an improved relationship. But a strong part of him remained skeptical. Herb had been hurt too many times before to be able to trust his mother completely.

Men in my therapy groups focus much more on their fathers than their mothers. This has to do in part with the importance of fathers in male social development. But I think it also has to do in part with men's relationships with their own mothers. I myself have been working on that relationship for the past fifteen years. Reconnecting with my mother has been a crucial component of my personal journey. I have come to understand her much better, and getting to know her has enabled me to improve my relationship with my wife and to be more sympathetic to women in general.

Although my mother is a source of emotional support and my number one booster, at times I find the attention a bit too much and would prefer her to be more focused on herself and her own accomplishments, which are considerable. But I'm learning. Now when I call her, or say goodbye, I am comfortable saying, "I love you." It feels good.

Perhaps it's easier to work on our personal relationships with our fathers because no matter what we do with them, they're unlikely to become too emotional. Mothers tend to be less predictable; they're likely to feel hurt, to push back. But it's time to stop taking our mothers for granted. We have to ask ourselves how it will feel when she's no longer there to ask us how we're doing, to offer us food, to cajole us, to compliment us, to ask the difficult questions, to wish us happy birthday, to inquire about our health — in short to show us how much she cares.

MEN AS FATHERS

At long last we were on vacation. After four cold, damp Michigan winter months we were at Hilton Head Island, with a tennis court right out the back door. My wife and I were going to play doubles against our eleven- and fifteen-year-old sons, who had been taking tennis lessons all winter.

Adam and Daniel were warming up when I came out to the court. My wife, Pat, was inside getting ready. I asked Adam to move down the court with Daniel so I could warm up. I wasn't aware of being tense, but when he said, "Why don't you hit with Dan on your end, and I'll stay here on my end," I saw red. And when Daniel agreed, I was pissed.

"You guys have already been warming up, and I need the practice. Move down to the other side of the net," I yelled.

More protest was all I needed to launch the attack. "You guys are getting spoiled. Don't you realize who's paying for your tennis lessons? Now get on down there, or you won't play at all." Even though they trudged to the other end, I didn't feel much better as I hit the first practice shot to Adam. He wound up and swung so hard the ball flew past my head and into the back fence.

I didn't know whether to scream or charge after him over the net. Instead I threw down my racket and stormed off the court. Puffing like a dragon and kicking dirt, I waited for him to come to apologize. It never even occurred to me that I may have owed them an apology.

After a few minutes he did come and apologize, but it was one of those "sorry, but . . ." types, which ended with a complaint about my rudeness. After the set (they won, of course) I was still feeling bad about what had happened. As I discussed it with my wife, it finally occurred to me that maybe my behavior was out of line. I wouldn't have told a friend in a similar situation to move over. Maybe I was just asserting my dominance.

A few hours later Adam and I went for a jog on the beach. As we paused to catch our breath, I told Adam I was sorry about the tennis. It wasn't polite to demand that he move over so I could warm up.

Adam seemed stunned. I asked why he looked so surprised. "Dad," he said, "that's the first time I ever remember winning an argument with you."

Now I was stunned. Could it be true? I had always thought of myself as such a fair, understanding father. Surely I had given in to him many times before.

"Yeah, you've given in, but this is the first time you've admitted you were wrong without giving me a lecture about what I had done wrong."

Despite our best efforts it really is difficult to be the kind of parent we want to be. Even with cognitive insight and emotional sensitivity, even with heroic efforts to come to terms with our own parents, we readily slip back into parenting patterns that we hated when growing up and that we swore we would never repeat.

Being a good father is the most complex challenge we face. I have no illusions that in a few brief pages I can even begin to address the subtleties and perplexities of the issue. What I do offer are some guidelines, gleaned from my own experience as a clinician and a father.

1. Be involved in your baby's birth. There is no more profound experience. Once you have seen that child emerge, and have held him or her, you will be bound to that child forever.

2. Recognize that you do matter to your children. A father is crucial to a child's health and happiness. Being there for that child is the most important thing you can do with your life.

3. Decide what kind of a father you want to be, and then go for it. You are free to be the kind of father you wish your father had been. How do you want to be different from your father? Which of his fathering talents do you wish to hold on to?

4. Consider not just what you can do for your child but what raising your child can do for you. Child rearing is an opportunity for liberation from childhood pain and an opportunity to re-create yourself, a chance to get it right this time.

5. Think of what kind of help you need to be the kind of father you want to be. You can't do it alone. As men we have not been trained to be good fathers.

Who can you talk to for advice? Where can you go for classes? What books can you read? Who will listen to your uncertainties?

6. Be aware of your areas of vulnerability and get help with them. We all have our Achilles' heels as parents. Know yours, admit them, and learn not to let them get in your way. What is it? Temper, impatience, arrogance, ignorance about children? Whatever it is, find it, identify it, and deal with it before it wrecks your relationship with your children.

7. Commit time to parenting. You can't be a good absent father. Your conscious presence, attention, and time are required.

8. Spend large chunks of time alone with your child. Don't be only a co-parent, a mother's helper. From the time your child is an infant until he leaves home, take some quality time each week to be a single parent.

9. Establish rituals with your child. Be sure to schedule regular activities together, both in the house and out of the house, one to one, just you and each child separately.

10. Make a conscious decision about physical punishment. I advise you never to use it, but if you insist, establish firm guidelines and never exceed them.

11. Don't hide behind your mask. Allow your children to know all of you, including your feelings and vulnerabilities. Show them you are a whole man, not a shadow.

12. Avoid the domineering father role.

13. Raise gender-sensitive children. Let them know that it's OK with you if they don't conform to narrow stereotypes about being boys or girls.

14. Keep your children out of disagreements with your spouse. Don't draw them in as allies or try to turn them against their other parent.

15. If you have abandoned a child, find him or her, and let him or her know you care. It's never too late.

16. Be positive. Avoid the criticism trap, which is when you almost always find fault with your child. Praise, praise, praise, and tell 'em you love 'em.

8 STAYING AWAKE: THE IMPORTANCE OF FRIENDSHIP

Although Nick and I are from different backgrounds and have pursued different career paths (he went to Vietnam and is now a small business owner; I went from college to teaching in Harlem and then became a psychologist), he is one of my few friends left from high school. These days, even though he lives less than fifty miles away, I see Nick only about once a year. When I called him recently to offer him and his son tickets to a basketball game, he quickly accepted. I was really looking forward to his visit, especially because I had not yet met his son, Shane, whom he and his wife recently adopted.

After a rushed pizza dinner, Nick and I finally had a few minutes alone before the game while our boys played downstairs. As is characteristic of Nick, he didn't waste any time. He clearly had something he wanted to say to me, and he jumped right into it.

"Rob, we've known each other for a long time, and you know I have the greatest respect for you," he said. "But I wonder about something. I know you're a therapist and all, but it's occurred to me that I never really hear you talk much about yourself. You're great about getting other people to open up, but I don't know that much about what's going on with you. You seem always to be on top of things, always cheerful. As you know, I've been through a lot of stuff in my life and so have many of our friends from high school. But I've never heard much about your stuff. It makes me wonder, have you ever gone through a crisis? What's going on inside you?"

I was listening nervously and intently. Right away I knew exactly what Nick was getting at. I admitted to him that he had picked up on a part of myself I still don't know how to handle. When it comes to friendship, I tend to hide behind my professional mask. I read *How to Win Friends and Influence People* in high school and learned how to be a good listener. But when it comes to revealing myself, I either address my work or joke about my problems. I've always had a difficult time revealing my problems, talking about my struggles, or admitting my uncertainties, a tendency related to being an only child. Without siblings to help me learn about the subtleties of interaction, I've always struggled to try to figure out how to fit in. Being upbeat, funny, and a good listener worked for me. Being self-revealing, even though it is a strategy I frequently recommend to my clients, is not a path with which I always feel comfortable.

I wanted to thank Nick for his honesty, but I stumbled in my response. "Nick," I concluded, "I appreciate your talking about this. I guess I've had my share of grief and pain just like you, but I don't tell many people about it. I confide in my wife and one close friend, but for the most part, I tend to keep things to myself."

Nick responded in one of the most caring ways I had ever experienced. "Rob, I'm saying this because I want to be better friends with you. I care about you. But being good friends is a two-way street. The last time we had lunch, I did all of the talking. I walked away and was mad. I had poured my heart out, yet I heard nothing about you."

In the few minutes we had left before the game, I talked more to Nick about myself than I probably had in all of the previous twenty-eight years of our friendship. Toward the end of the conversation I told him how much I appreciated his feedback. It had been honest, and he presented it to me as an invitation to get closer, not an accusation. It had been a wonderful gift, something I have always longed for — honest feedback from a friend about how he sees me and how he would like to see our friendship grow.

WHY FRIENDSHIP IS SO IMPORTANT FOR MEN

In deciding to make the topic of friendship the book's final chapter, I am acknowledging that reconnecting with old friends and making and maintaining new ones is an essential ingredient in men's growth and development. Let me set down some of the reasons why I consider friendship so important.

In order to take proper care of ourselves, we must eat wisely, exercise often, and get proper rest. But that's not enough. To keep our emotional selves in shape, we must work to maintain our friendships. Friendship is vital to our health and happiness and is an important factor in the reduction of stress. Several recent studies have shown that people who have intimate friendships are more likely to survive heart attacks and less likely to develop cancer and serious infections. There is a strong correlation between a lack of social relationships and high blood pressure, cigarette smoking, and obesity.

Without close friendships, men lose perspective on what is simply part of being a man at various stages of our lives. Several men have entered one of my men's groups with the express intention of trying to understand what is normal behavior for men at midlife. Lacking close male friends, we have no one to compare ourselves with on an open and honest basis.

When it comes to midlife crisis, the lack of perspective is particularly confusing. Most men recognize that a midlife crisis is an expected part of maturing, yet when it hits, it still catches many men unaware. All of a sudden a man finds himself infatuated with a younger woman and is dreaming of a new life with her. Without other men to talk to about his feelings, he has nowhere to turn. To discuss it with his wife is unthinkable. If he could talk to other men, he might realize how common such an infatuation is. He would learn how others have handled it without destroying their lives. But if he has no close friends, he keeps his fantasies a secret. The secrets eventually turn to deceitful behavior, and the crisis broadens.

Without close friends, we become lonely. With the pressures on men to make a living and to provide for the family, little time is available for friendship. As a consequence, men long for the sense of connectedness with other males that they probably last experienced in high school or college. As one of my friends said, "It's tough to make new friends in adulthood." The popularity of "men's gatherings" is an indication of how much men long for the company of other men.

Yet men have grown so used to going it alone that they may not even recognize their feelings of loneliness. Without close male friends, a man tends to become excessively dependent on the woman in his life, whom he often views as his best friend. This puts a tremendous strain on their relationship and leaves him resourceless if this relationship ends. A recent survey showed that a "whole two-thirds of men name their wives as their best friends, while only 40% of women return the compliment." Many men do not even tell their friends that they are getting divorced.

Without close friendships, we also become disconnected from the past. In a mobile society people tend to move away from the neighborhoods where they grew up. Our close friends from grade school, high school, or college tend to get lost in the shuffle between jobs and communities. If you stop to think (or feel) about it, there are probably many boyhood friends you'd love to call or write. Why do we hesitate?

For many men it simply feels too awkward. Ted, a recent client of mine, talked about longing to see old friends when he returned to his hometown for a Christmas visit. In therapy he talked about how important those friends had been to him and how much he missed them. When I encouraged him to look them up on his visit, he balked. "No, I wouldn't want to impose on them," he said wistfully. Fortunately in this case I was able to convince him otherwise.

As we get older we must also realize that these old friends are not always going to be there for us to visit. This was brought home to me a few years ago when I stopped by to visit Dave, one of my college roommates. Dave asked me about Craig, the third roommate. "I haven't talked to Craig in years," I responded, "but let's see if we can find him." We looked in the phone book and found him easily, living in the next town over from Dave. I picked up the phone and called.

Craig was delighted to hear from us but surprised by our timing. Two weeks earlier he had been diagnosed with testicular cancer. Since he was to start treatment the next day, he wanted to get together with us that very afternoon. The three of us and our wives all went to see *The Big Chill*, which was about us — a group of students at the University of Michigan in the 1960s. We wept through the movie and had a wonderful reunion dinner afterward.

Three months later Craig died from complications from the chemotherapy. This longtime friend, the only American on the Michigan hockey team in 1968, had died before his fortieth birthday. The loss served to remind me how important our friends are, and I was grateful for the chance to have had a heartwarming visit with him before he died.

OBSTACLES

Despite the strong incentives to reduce their loneliness, most men find it difficult to make and maintain friendships. The causes for this are rooted in our professionally competitive society, which emphasizes the accumulation of wealth, prestige, and power. These values put a strain on friendships, which require cooperation, equal status, and the sharing of vulnerabilities and unpleasant truths. Stated simply, it is extremely difficult to develop a close, trusting friendship with a potential competitor. Does it make sense to share your vulnerabilities with someone who might use them to his advantage for a job promotion?

Competition is an inhibiting factor with old friends as well. When a client, Ray, asked one of his old friends, Jim, why he had not returned his letters and phone calls, Jim gave him an interesting response: "Ray, my life hasn't been going so great lately," he said. "A few months ago I lost my job." Ray was shocked. Why hadn't Jim let him know about his crisis? In discussing it further with Jim, Ray figured out that Jim felt embarrassed at being down. While Jim's life was on the skids, Ray's life, it seemed to Jim, was going splendidly. While they stayed on relatively equal grounds, their friendship had remained stable. But when their fortunes went in different directions, Jim felt ashamed. He no longer saw himself as Ray's equal. He felt the need to withdraw and hide his hurts.

Ray was eventually able to reach out and support Jim, but the lesson was a painful one for both of them. At a time of great need, the two friends had been initially unable to connect in a meaningful way.

Certainly there are many obstacles to male friendships, but in my clinical experience the competitive nature of our society is the single most important obstacle. It makes us distrust other men, because we fear that they will take advantage of us in our weaker moments. Men tend to think of friends as "contacts" who might be able to help us further our career goals, rather than as true friends, people we just enjoy being around. Our tendency is to keep score in relationships — to see who is doing better, making more money, achieving more honors, and so forth.

The story of Frank and Ron is a good example of how difficult it is for men to sustain a friendship with someone they work with. Frank, my client, was a businessman who decided to start his own consulting firm. At first he did all the work on his own, but when business began to boom, he decided to ask his best friend, Ron, to help him out.

Frank and Ron had maintained a very special friendship for fifteen years, since their days in college. As a result, Frank and Ron did not take time early in their business relationship to clearly delineate the terms of their working arrangement. Perhaps their friendship made it awkward for them to talk specifically about financial arrangements.

Everything went along splendidly until it came time to make a key business decision. Frank believed he was the boss and that he had the right to make the decisions as he pleased. His friend was hurt. He believed that Frank had asked him to be his partner and that he should have equal say in the decision. Furthermore, Ron thought he should be receiving more recognition and more money for his contributions.

Without seeing it coming suddenly their new business relationship had put a significant strain on their friendship. Frank was extremely upset. He feared losing the friendship but also was uncomfortable giving Ron what he wanted.

Although they had been able to reach a compromise on the business issues, even a year after the incident there were still traces of discomfort between them. They had grown a little wary, a little distrustful of each other. When they could not resolve their differences on their own, Frank suggested to Ron that they come to see me to try to ease the tension between them. Ron agreed.

In the session they talked about the history of their friendship and began to recognize how their personal histories had affected their relationship in unexpected ways. A middle child, Ron had always looked to his older brother for guidance. But when his brother died in an auto accident, he felt terribly alone. At about that time Ron and Frank's friendship began growing stronger. Without realizing it, Ron transferred some of his expectations for guidance from his deceased brother to his new friend, Frank.

As Ron opened up, so did Frank. As an only child he had always longed for a brother. Ron had come to be that brother. Yet being an only child had instilled in him a sense of having to go it alone, having to make his way on his own merits. As a consequence he had become somewhat insensitive to the needs and feelings of others.

Frank recognized that Ron had been right about many aspects of the business problem. In his eagerness to make the business a success, he had not paused to think how it would affect his best friend. He thought he had been doing Ron a favor. Instead he realized he was putting their friendship in danger.

Their talk was extremely moving. By the end of the session all of us were in tears. They each acknowledged having learned a powerful lesson the hard way. Even the best of male friendships is extremely vulnerable to our tendency to compete. Working together can put such strain on friends that the friendship and the work partnership may inevitably be incompatible.

Even though the incident put a terrible strain on Frank and Ron's relationship, in the end they were able to overcome it by being truthful with each other about their feelings and by taking seriously their commitment to each other. Even so they both learned how perilous friendship between men can be. Unlike marriage, no vow keeps two friends connected. Only their feelings, needs, and willingness to suspend male pride enable their friendship to endure.

Men Hurting Men.   Most men have been hurt by other men's jabs, which are ostensibly for fun but actually reinforce a hostile hierarchy. These experiences create wariness and distrust of other men, which present serious obstacles to the development of intimate male friendship.

Among the most common ways to inflict pain is through teasing. To be part of the male culture a man must learn to tease and to take the teasing of others. Some extremely cruel comments can be made in the guise of a tease. Yet to play the game correctly, a man knows the appropriate response is always to counter with another teasing remark. If a man reveals that the teasing bothers him, he is labeled as too sensitive; if he gets angry at the teasing, he is labeled a hothead.

If we ask the one teasing us to clarify his remark, he invariably replies, "Oh, I was just kidding. I didn't mean anything by it." But Freud argued that there really are no jokes; they are simply a more socially acceptable way to vent hostility.

Frequently the intent of teasing is to shame the recipient. Men seem to develop a hypersensitive radar that enables us to pick up the flaws, vulnerabilities, and mistakes of other men. When we sense that another man is faltering, we have learned to be swift in pointing it out to him. It's almost as if life is a one-on-one basketball game, each player ready to take advantage of his opponent's mistake to score a point.

Sometimes the competition between men is so powerful and pervasive that in quiet moments of truth a man will admit that part of him takes some perverse pleasure in his friend's misfortune. If he hears, for example, that his friend is having marital difficulties and his own marriage is going relatively smoothly (at this moment), he feels some sense of satisfaction. While on the surface he may express sympathy, on another level a part of him might say, "Well, at least I know how to get along with women better than Fred does." This is not a conscious evaluation. It comes automatically, the result of years of training and conditioning that have taught us to evaluate ourselves in relation to other men.

The converse is also true. If a friend experiences success, part of a man feels behind because the friend, at least at that moment, is doing better than he is. This obsession with keeping score results in keeping distant. If we cannot take full pleasure in the achievement of a friend because of our automatic envy, then we can never get really close to that friend. The progression is fixed: comparison leads to envy; envy leads to distance.

Sports is another social mechanism for teaching men to evaluate ourselves against other men. Although participation in sports can be an important developmental experience, it can also leave a foul-tasting residue. Sports are, of course, based on competition and are usually zero-sum games; that is, only one side can win, and the other must lose. As boys progress through the years, it becomes harder and harder to make the team. Sooner or later almost every boy experiences athletic failure or rejection.

The sports experience is made even more brutal emotionally by the attitude and tactics of the coach. All too often the stereotype of the coach is a reality: a negative, insensitive man who employs shaming and harassing, seemingly learned from Grade B marine movies. Over the years I have heard countless stories of men being humiliated by their coaches — being criticized, called names, even pushed or hit because they are not measuring up in the coach's eyes. The coach can, of course, be an important mentor. But so much pressure is placed on him to win that he resorts to whatever methods he knows to ensure that his players triumph.

Too many men leave sports feeling diminished. The team experience can provide a model for how to be close to other men, but often it is a model for how to compete against and be wary of other men or to feel excluded from their company.

Homophobia. The fear of homosexuality is another inhibitor of male friendship. It leads men to be wary of getting too close to other men. The fear of being perceived as homosexual inhibits physical affection between men, keeps them from appearing to care too much about other men, and in general creates an atmosphere of distrust and uncertainty between men. (For more on this see pp.158 – 163, chapter 6.)

Time Constraints. Many men tell me that so much of their time is dominated by work and family that they simply do not have enough left over for friendship. On some levels there may be some truth to this contention. A recent study shows that the average worker today devotes 20 percent more of his time to work than men did twenty years ago. Especially in the early 1990s, with economic pressures so great, men have relatively little leisure time. What time is left is often devoted to contributing to child care or housework. Job, wife, kids — these are the top three priorities, usually in that order, and little time remains for anything else.

Distance from Our Fathers.   The father-son relationship is the prototype for other relationships with men. If we cannot get close to our fathers, how are we to get close to other men? If we have been hurt by our fathers, how can we trust other men? If we have been abandoned by our fathers, how can we depend on other men?

Men who do not come to terms with their fathers may transfer their feelings from their fathers to other men. This is one other important reason why men need to work on their feelings toward and relationships with their fathers, as we discussed in the previous chapter.

GUIDELINES FOR DEVELOPING FRIENDSHIPS WITH MEN

Even though I am advocating developing closer male friendships as an important part of the awakening process, each reader must decide for himself how much he desires and needs to be closer to other men. Some people are more focused on developing affiliations than others. The following questions may help in the evaluation:

- Do you miss specific friends from your past and wish you could reconnect with them?

- At times of need is there a man you can talk to about your problems?

- Do you wish you had more buddies, people you could just go out with to have a good time?

- Are you wary and distrustful of the men you meet? Do you have difficulty opening up to male acquaintances?

Reconnecting with Old Friends.

Think of old friends from various times in your life whom you wish you could see again. Identify two or three you would most like to reconnect with in the next few years. Write a letter saying you would like to get back together. In the letter talk about yourself in an honest way, including something about the bumps and bruises you've experienced in your life. Avoid assuming a one-up, "everything's fine" posture.

If you believe that there might be unresolved hurts between you, mention them in the letter and express your desire to get past them. If you think you may have hurt your friend in the past, apologize. End the letter by suggesting specific times to get together and activities you two might do together.

If you're not a letter writer, a friendly phone call may do the trick. Despite Ma Bell's commercials that indicate otherwise, most men are not too comfortable on the phone. But do your best to be warm and enthusiastic. End the call with an attempt to make some specific plan about getting together in the future. Calling up with tickets to a special event is a good way to get started.

If you have an old friend whom you do see but with whom you'd like to become closer, plan ways to try to open up the relationship: plan a trip together — to fish, hike, visit museums, or whatever it is you two enjoy doing together; talk about some part of yourself that you tend to hide from others — take a risk on making yourself vulnerable to your friend; talk directly about your friendship — how does he see you, how do you see him, how would each of you like to see the friendship improved?

Any friendship is strengthened by attentiveness. Remember his birthday; call occasionally just to talk; ask about his family of origin; send him clippings that may be of interest to him; if you know he's been sick or had a problem, contact him to see how he's doing.

You can also contact him at times when you are needy. Perhaps you're worried about your job; maybe your parents are sick or you've had an argument with your wife. At these times when men tend to withdraw, try to accept help from your friends. They're almost always flattered, and eventually they will reciprocate, although not always right away.

If your friend lives out of town, go visit him or suggest that you would like to meet him halfway. Don't worry about intruding in his life. It's his responsibility (and loss) if he wants to say no. Most callers are surprised to discover that their old friends are thrilled to hear from them. Chances are, they may be stuck in the same rut about friendships that you are.

Making New Friends

If you decide that developing friendships is an important priority, but you have not been able to do it, can you identify the personal obstacles that get in your way? This may help you discern your obstacles.

Fear of rejection

Unresolved conflicts with old friends

Insufficient time

Excessive competitiveness with other men

Preference for the company of women

Preference to be alone

Homophobia

Your wife's opposition

Inability to find any men to be friends with

Past failures in your attempts to make friends

Recognize from the start that it will take a concerted effort to make new friends. It is necessary to set aside your male ego, because you are likely to experience some rejection or indifference along the way. It helps to remember that this is something you are doing for yourself, not an attempt to "be liked." It is not a test of popularity but an effort on your part to take better care of yourself by doing something about your need to be connected with other men.

Join in some regularly scheduled activities where you are likely to meet men you might want to befriend. Most friendships between men develop indirectly; you are involved together in some activity — a team, work, a volunteer organization, a class, your kids' team. As you meet regularly, you talk. Eventually suggest doing something together away from the activity — a beer after the game, for example, or getting together with your kids and his to go to a playground.

It helps to eventually set up regular times to get together. With people's schedules so busy, the only way to have a chance at developing the friendship is to make it a routine part of your schedule. Suggest having lunch monthly or buying season tickets together to some event, or ask a potential friend to join you on a project— taking a class, learning a new hobby, volunteering.

While together, try to open up about yourself. When he asks, "How are you doing?" give the rarest of things: an honest answer, not the whitewashed one. Tell him what you worry about in the middle of the night or what you dream of doing instead of going into work. Assume at first that you'll have to do most of the opening up. If reciprocity comes, it will be slow.

Some men find it helpful to keep their wives out of it (at least until the friendship is well established). Many times as soon as two men start to become good friends, they feel compelled to get together as a foursome with their wives. This puts the budding friendship in danger because if any of the new combinations of people do not like each other, the friendship will be greatly stressed. Eventually you may become friends as couples or families, but remember that your primary goal is to develop a friendship for yourself. Naturally, finding four people who enjoy one another is much more complicated than finding two. I also believe that men often want to pull wives into a friendship because they feel more comfortable with social intimacy when their wives are present.

After the friendship is established, the guidelines are similar to those for connecting with old friends: be attentive; plan outings together; be a good listener but also share yourself.

An essential trait of strong friendships is openness in times of conflict or disappointment in the relationship. Many a friendship begins promisingly, only to crash-land because conflict develops without being addressed. Rather than discuss what is bothering us, we take our ball and go home. Owing to human nature, conflicts and disagreements will arise, and you can expect them in your new friendships. The trick is to handle the occasional friction openly and maturely.

If friendship between men is to grow, you must make a commitment to each other to talk about things that are bothering you. These can include perceived slights, misinterpreted remarks, and differences of opinion. Simply to lick your wounds and try to tough it out drives a wedge between the two of you, which just gets wider with time.

OTHER TYPES OF MEANINGFUL RELATIONSHIPS WITH MEN

The Mentor

The one topic of Robert Bly's best-selling book *Iron John* that men seem most attracted to is the need to be mentored and to mentor others. The mentorship role is a complicated one, because it inevitably entails an unequal distribution of power. Yet finding or being a mentor can also be one of the most rewarding roles a man can experience. I encourage the reader to consider finding a mentor relationship as another important way to maintain self-awareness. Much of what we have discussed about friendship applies to mentorship.

I believe that in this type of relationship special caution must be exercised in order to ensure that the mentor does not abuse his power. Some men look back on their mentors with mixed feelings: On the one hand they are grateful for the help and learning they received; but on the other hand they feel that the mentor took unfair advantage of the situation, sometimes by using his protégés work to advance his own career or by asking the protégé to serve him in demeaning ways. These situations can be easily avoided if one is reasonably aware of the possibility. Don't let apprehensions about such a situation arising, however, keep you from exploring this kind of relationship.

The Volunteer

In an age when society's problems seem almost insurmountable, becoming a volunteer can be an extremely satisfying endeavor. Furthermore, it is also beneficial to your health. A recent study of longevity found that volunteerism was the single most important factor in predicting who lived longest. Apparently giving of your time to others on a volunteer basis has some distinct advantages that we may have overlooked. The opportunities for volunteering are many, including coaching, tutoring, leading a Boy Scout troop, or becoming a Big Brother, to name a few.

Participating in a Men's Group

Throughout this book I have talked about the importance of men's groups. In this final section I present ideas on how to join or form a men's group. The unifying focus in all men's groups is our experience of being male. Within that framework is wide variation on how men's groups are organized and worked.

Some groups are based on the recovery, or Twelve-Step, model. The group format follows the principles of Alcoholics Anonymous, which are spelled out in detail in the *Big Book of AA*. Today these groups include Sex Addicts Anonymous, Codependents Anonymous, Adult Children of Alcoholics, and Narcotics Anonymous, among others. Most local newspapers carry a weekly list of these groups, which are leaderless and free of charge.

Therapist-led Groups. In these groups, like the ones described throughout this book, a therapist functions as the group facilitator. A fee is usually charged in these groups, which are similar to group therapy except that all of the members are male. They may be open-ended (no prearranged number of meetings) or time limited.

Leaderless Men's Support Groups. These groups generally have been started by a group of acquaintances or may be sponsored by an organized group, such as a church or synagogue. The men in the group either rotate the leadership or have no designated leader. The only fee involved is that required for the maintenance of group activities, such as mailings and food.

Several groups like this have been in existence since the 1970s. They vary considerably in terms of format, focus, and intent. Some focus on a mythic-poetic model, which is based on the perspective of Robert Bly and emphasizes ritual drumming, story telling, and the search for the "deep masculine." Others focus on political action and men's consciousness raising. There are also are gay rights or gay awareness groups. There are groups that focus on the specific problems or concerns of the members, but from the particular perspective of men and masculinity.

Even though leaderless men's groups have been around for a long time, they are not easy to find. Some larger cities have men's coordinating councils, but for the most part participants are found by word of mouth. Attending a men's weekend retreat is an excellent way to tap into the men's network in your area and to learn about opportunities for participation in men's groups.

There's nothing to stop you from starting your own men's group. One way is through networking with friends. Ask some men you know if they would be interested, and ask each of them to bring another friend or two.

Another approach is to start a men's group through an organization to which you belong. Several of us who are members of a temple, for example, started a men's group that has now been in existence for two years. We began by putting a notice in the temple bulletin and by spreading the news word of mouth. We set a regular meeting time (the second and fourth Sundays of each month) so everyone would remember. We now have about twenty people in the group, of which a shifting dozen or so seem to participate each time. Leadership rotates based on who proposes the topic for the next meeting.

One key to the group's cohesiveness is a biweekly letter that one of the members sends out before each meeting. We all look forward to the bright yellow sheet arriving in the mail. It's a great way to be reminded of the meeting.

Over the course of its two years our group has addressed a variety of fascinating topics, from friendship, fathers, and money to mentors, midlife career choices, religion, health, sexuality, and aging. We have maintained certain standards for our group process, such as getting past our masks to our emotions, dealing directly with conflict, and guarding confidentiality. The group experience has been important to our development as men. Even though the group is not always intense, and even though it has not always led to the development of close friendships between group members, it has been an invaluable experience for all of us. When I first listed the reasons why, it read like a recapitulation of all that has been discussed in this book:

- It has helped us overcome our sense of social isolation.
- It has enabled us to see that as men we are not so different from one another as we feared.
- It has enabled us to appreciate how profound an influence male socialization has had on the way we think, feel, and believe.
- It has afforded us the opportunity to talk honestly and directly with other men.
- It has enabled us to tap our feelings and to accept them as legitimate parts of ourselves.
- It has given us insight into our families of origin.
- It has helped us define what kind of men we want to be.
- It has helped us to stop blaming women and to start taking responsibility for ourselves.
- It has taught us to be more caring, nurturing, and supportive of other men.
- It has given us hope for the future.

THE PAYOFF

Explaining the benefits of male friendship is one thing; showing you is another. You remember Nick, the old friend I introduced at the beginning of this chapter, who leveled with me before the basketball game. Two days after our talk, I received this letter from him.

Dear Rob,

Just wanted to drop you a short note and thank you for dinner and the tickets to the basketball game. Michigan started out poorly but took it to them in the second half.

I just finished reading a letter you wrote me in July of 1969, when you were living at 316 West 93rd in New York. You mentioned how good it was to see me and Jeff [another high school friend], right before I left for Viet Nam.

Somehow we all went different directions and stopped being friends. I didn't see Jeff for several years after that. Finally, after coming back from Nam, I cornered him and asked him what the hell had happened? He told me he felt badly for everything I went through. I proceeded to tell him that was bullshit, that we would always be friends and share many, many memories together. He has since told me that he wishes he had some good friends in D.C., but you can't make friends like the people you grew up with.

When I saw you at the top of the stairs with your dog the other night, I truly wanted to go up and give you a big hug. As we get older, I think we become more guarded and don't want to show our true emotions, and we certainly don't want to appear weak or vulnerable.

In your new book please mention the importance of being open and sharing. The only true bridge to real friendship is being vulnerable; then and only then do you start to build lasting friendships.

It seems like yesterday you and your wife were going to be famous actors, and instead you're both psychologists. But Jeff hasn't really changed that much, and you haven't either. Even though we may have problems from time to time, and even change directions, you can't take away our friendship and memories. We will always be old school buddies. Remember that you will always have a friend here.

Nick

100 Ways to Stay Awake

1. Restore balance in your life.

2. Keep track daily of the abundances in your life.

3. On your daily calendar record TGCOY: what you do each day to take good care of yourself (jog, meditate, write in journal, etc.).

4. Develop a spiritual practice.

5. Call at least one friend weekly.

6. Join a men's group.

7. Read women's literature to try to better understand the women's movement.

8. Learn a new sport that you can do even into old age.

9. Plan a trip for your family.

10. Plan a trip with men friends.

11. Get involved in a project to improve life on earth.

12. Set up regular times to do things one-on-one with your children.

13. Set daily goals that have nothing to do with work.

14. Set up regular lunch times with a friend.

15. Take daily walks with your wife.

16. Get a dog.

17. Start a small garden.

18. Have lunch out with each of your children at least once a month.

19. Find a barber you like, and get to know him or her well.

20. Thank God (or someone) for the blessings of each day.

21. Be more positive with everyone.

22. Give yourself a break.

23. Plan some solitude. Go away by yourself at least one weekend a year.

24. Do something you're afraid of.

25. Make fanciful lists.

26. Read biographies of people you admire (not just great ones).

27. Watch sunrises and sunsets.

28. Learn to cook one great thing for each meal of the day.

29. Buy nice blank cards and send them out routinely.

30. Stretch daily.

31. Give yourself credit for not losing your temper.

32. Identify all your subpersonalities (or parts of self).

33. Memorize a poem.

34. Become an expert on something.

35. Stand up to someone you're afraid of.

36. Learn to dance.

37. Call people up to congratulate them on their successes.

38. Develop a good relationship with a doctor. Get to know the doctor well enough so you're not afraid to talk about your health.

39. Get away with your wife for a couple's weekend.

40. Admit that you are powerless over certain things or people in your life. Appreciate them for teaching you humility.

41. Celebrate the arrival of each new season.

42. Tell the people who help you regularly how much you appreciate them.

43. Learn to live more in the moment.

44. Let your kids beat you in games.

45. Tell your kids you're sorry when you make a mistake.

46. Talk it out with someone you've been upset with.

47. Be loving. Don't take love for granted.

48. Ditto for health.

49. Do something nice for a neighbor.

50. Reconnect with relatives you haven't seen in years.

51. Frame some favorite pictures.

52. Write your own words on note cards instead of relying on Hallmark poets.

53. Teach your kids about nature by going out in it.

54. Listen to the stories in country music.

55. Teach yourself to meditate or relax in quietude.

56. Ask people about their family histories.

57. Love yourself just the way you are.

58. Find a mechanic you trust.

59. Count your blessings.

60. Feel the fear—and do whatever it is you're afraid of.

61. Try eating without reading.

62. Limit TV to the weekends.

63. When you're happy, enjoy it.

64. Let go of trying to control others.

65. Learn from your arguments.

66. Raise your kids as well as you possibly can.

67. Find women with whom you can be friends without being sexual.

68. How important is it to keep trying to earn more money?

69. Plan a career change.

70. Enjoy daily pleasures.

71. Talk to your mate about sex.

72. Enjoy yourself.

73. You can't change solely on your own.

74. You can get by with a little help from your friends.

75. Learn to take care of the world we live in.

76. Learn to take care of the body you live in.

77. Find an outlet for your creative spirit.

78. Learn to cry.

79. Be willing to terminate friendships that are a constant drag.

80. Tell people you appreciate them.

81. Realize that the journey is both within and without.

82. Hug someone in front of your kids.

83. Share your pain with someone you trust.

84. Unhitch yourself from the pursuit of money.

85. Learn to leave work stress at the office.

86. Slow down. Try to make the morning last.

87. Ask yourself, how much is enough?

88. Give yourself permission to be imperfect.

89. Learn to let go of outcome.

90. Work for political change that will make the workplace a healthier place for men and women.

91. Help the lost boys (boys without fathers).

92. In a conversation, ask a question and listen to the answer.

93. Initiate, plan, and carry through a social activity with your wife, including calling a babysitter.

94. Stay in the room when your mate starts to cry.

95. It's OK to say "I don't know."

96. Honor the teacher in you that will guide the next generation.

97. Teach your daughter how to use a power drill.

98. Trust your intuition.

99. Show a little tenderness.

100. Be a volunteer.

SUGGESTED READING

Akeret, Robert. *Family Tales, Family Wisdom.* New York: William Morrow, 1991.

Bass, Ellen, and Laura Davis. *The Courage to Heal: A Guide for Women Survivors of Child Sexual Abuse.* New York: Perennial Library/Harper & Row, 1988.

Bell, Donald. *Being a Man.* New York: Harcourt Brace Jovanovich, 1982.

Bepko, Claudia and Jo-Ann Krestin. *Too Good for Her Own Good.* New York: Harper & Row, 1990.

Bly, Robert. *Iron John.* Reading, MA: Addison-Wesley, 1990.

Bolen, Jean Shinoda. *Gods in Everyman.* New York: Harper & Row, 1989.

Carnes, Patrick. *Don't Call it Love: Recovery from Sexual Addiction.* New York: Bantam, 1991.

Comfort, Alex. *The New Joy of Sex.* New York: Crown Publishers, 1991.

Conroy, Pat. *Prince of Tides.* Boston: Houghton Mifflin, 1986.

Eisler, Riane. *The Chalice and the Blade: Our History, Our Future.* San Francisco: Harper & Row, 1988.

Faludi, Susan. *Backlash: The Undeclared War Against American Women.* New York: Crown Publishers, 1991.

Farrell, Warren. *Why Men Are the Way They Are.* New York: McGraw Hill, 1986.

Fossum, Merle. *Catching Fire.* San Francisco: Harper/Hazelden, 1989.

Fossum, Merle, and Marilyn Mason. *Facing Shame.* New York: W. W. Norton, 1986.

Gilligan, Carol. *In a Different Voice.* Cambridge, MA: Harvard Univ. Press, 1983.

Gilmore, David D. *Manhood in the Making*. New Haven: Yale Univ. Press, 1990.

Goldberg, Herbert. *The New Male*. New York: Signet, 1979.

Grevin, Philip. *Spare the Child*. New York: Alfred A. Knopf, 1991.

Groening, Matt. *Childhood Is Hell*. New York: Pantheon, 1988.

Hochschild, Arlie. *The Second Shift*. New York: Avon, 1989.

Kauth, Bill. *Men's Friends: How to Organize and Run Your Own Men's Support Group*. Milwaukee: Human Development Associates, 1991.

Keen, Sam. *Fire in the Belly*. New York: Bantam, 1991.

Kohn, Alfie. *No Contest: The Case Against Competition*. Boston: Houghton Mifflin, 1986.

Lee, John. *Flying Boy*. Deerfield Beach, FL: Health Communications, 1987.

Lerner, Harriet Goldhor. *The Dance of Anger*. New York: Harper & Row, 1986.

Levinson, Daniel. *The Seasons of a Man's Life*. New York: Ballantine Books, 1978.

Lew, Michael. *Victims No Longer*. New York: Nevraumont Publishing, 1988.

Marlin, Emily. *Genograms*. Chicago and New York: Contemporary Books, 1989.

Mason, Marilyn. *Making Our Lives Our Own*. San Francisco: Harper San Francisco, 1991.

Meth, Richard, and Robert Pasick. *Men in Therapy: The Challenge of Change*. New York: Guilford Press, 1990.

Miller, Jean Baker. *Toward a New Psychology of Women*. Boston: Beacon Press, 1986.

Miller, Stuart. *Men and Friendship*. San Leandro, CA: Gateway Books, 1983.

Moore, Robert, and Douglas Gillette. *King, Warrior, Magician, Lover, Poet*. San Francisco: Harper San Francisco, 1990.

Napier, Augustus. *The Fragile Bond*. New York: Harper & Row, 1988.

Osherson, Samuel. *Finding Our Fathers*. New York: Fawcett Columbine, 1986.

Pittman, Frank. *Private Lies*. New York: W.W. Norton, 1988.

Reinisch, June, and Ruth Beasley. *The Kinsey Institute New Report on Sex*. New York: St. Martin's Press, 1990.

Roth, Philip. *Patrimony*. New York: Simon & Schuster, 1991.

Schaef, Anne Wilson. *Co-dependence: Misunderstood-Mistreated*. San Francisco: Harper & Row, 1986.

Schor, Juliet. *The Overworked American: The Unexpected Decline of Leisure*. New York: Basic Books, 1991.

Stoltenberg, John. *Refusing to Be a Man*. New York: Penguin USA/Meredian, 1990.

Tannen, Deborah. *You Just Don't Understand*. New York: William Morrow, 1990.

Walker, Alice. *In Search of Our Mother's Gardens*. New York: Harcourt Brace Jovanovich, 1983.

Wilson, August. *Fences*. New York: Plume, 1986.